cooking with herbs

cooking with herbs

50 Simple Recipes for Fresh Flavor

Lynn Alley

Photography by Dhanraj Emanuel

**Andrews McMeel
Publishing, LLC**

Kansas City · Sydney · London

Andrews McMeel Publishing, LLC
an Andrews McMeel Universal company
1130 Walnut Street, Kansas City, Missouri 64106
www.andrewsmcmeel.com

13 14 15 16 17 TEN 10 9 8 7 6 5 4 3 2 1

ISBN: 978-1-4494-2769-6

Library of Congress Control Number: 2012949684

Photography by Dhanraj Emanuel
Design and illustrations by Julie Barnes

ATTENTION: SCHOOLS AND BUSINESSES
Andrews McMeel books are available at quantity discounts with bulk purchase for educational, business, or sales promotional use. For information, please e-mail the Andrews McMeel Publishing Special Sales Department: specialsales@amuniversal.com

Acknowledgments

To my lifelong friend, Ranjit Singh Gil, who first shared his love of gardening with me many years ago when we were students. To my very dear friend and neighbor, Kathy Fleming, of Accomplishment Coaching, who is always the coach, whether in the office, the kitchen, or at the table. To Dhanraj Emanuel with so many thanks for your patience and beautiful photographs. To Joe Bennion, a unique Spring City, Utah, potter whose work, words, and life have inspired me. To M., as always.

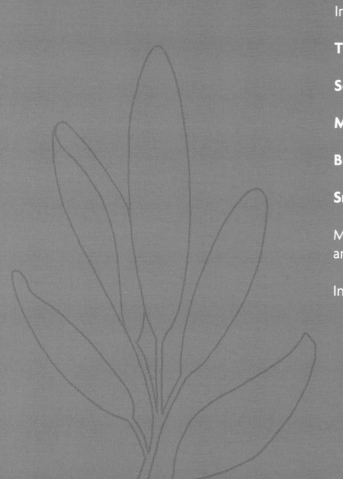

Introduction

When I was a child, my mother kept a shelf in the kitchen cabinet devoted to dried herbs. The old Schilling red-and-white cans. I knew a few names, but had no idea how to use them or what their distinguishing characteristics might be. I was far more interested in the chocolate chips she kept hidden behind them than in the herbs themselves.

My high school English teacher, Laurie Staude, was the first to draw my attention to fresh herbs. I admired her. She carried on at some length one day about an "omelet sprinkled with fresh-picked rosemary." I did not know what an omelet was, but I could use my imagination. So I headed off to a Renaissance Pleasure Faire in the hills of Marin County that had a gypsy wagon selling small herbs in pots. I bought a rosemary plant and carefully carried it home, set it in my bedroom window, and tended it with loving care. Then I chopped the first of its leaves and sprinkled them over a poached egg, believing that perhaps *this* was an omelet.

My second encounter was also with rosemary. A college friend and I were traveling from California to the Grand Canyon during spring break and I was doing the roadside cooking. We stopped at a gas station somewhere near Kingman, Arizona, and I noticed some scruffy plants around the periphery of the gas station. They smelled like rosemary, so I took some cuttings and used them on that night's chicken dinner. Delish!

A couple of years later, when I had a garden with some space behind my college house, I actually planted an herb and vegetable garden all of my own. (I will not forget the very first dish I made from my garden treasures: a soup of cabbage, tomatoes, and rosemary.)

By that time, I had become interested in both the medicinal and the culinary uses of herbs, so I had great fun cooking and mixing herbal decoctions for colds and flu.

Jump forward a few years and I was living in Southern California, leading tours, teaching herb cooking classes, and catering herb lunches at the largest herb nursery in the United States. Very little in this world could compare to a saunter through the mother garden on a warm day. Aromas of rosemary, oregano, sage, and more exotic herbs would rise up to meet me as I brushed against them. What a beautiful place it was! My lunches were redolent with juicy, herb-filled recipes and were ultimately laid out picnic style on the large rolling lawn that sloped down to the pond. Many of the recipes I developed then are still in my repertoire today; in fact, you might even find some of them in this book.

Truth be known, the garden itself was the inspiration for my cooking. Rather than choosing main ingredients around which to build a dish, I chose my herb or herbs from what looked good on any given day, then built my dish around them. As one of my culinary heroes, Angelo Pellegrini, wrote in his book *The Food Lover's Garden,*

The garden becomes, as it has for me, a veritable arsenal of culinary suggestions. As you survey what you have grown, and come to know their individual and collective virtues, they suggest what use you may make of them on any given day to produce a good dinner. I know whereof I speak, for I have learned to listen to mine. And they have never disappointed me.

As I look back over the years, I can see the ways in which herbs have woven themselves in and out of my life. Even today, I continue to enjoy them in the garden, the kitchen, and even in flower arrangements throughout the house.

A WORD ABOUT HERBS

First, a distinction: The term *herb* is used for the green parts (leaves) of aromatic plants, whereas the term *spice* refers to woody plant parts and seeds, such as cinnamon (bark) or coriander seed.

No one knows for sure why herbs developed such strong smells and flavors, but scientists have surmised that the sometimes bitter, aromatic oils that develop in little pods on the surface of the leaves are a natural insect repellent. In addition, these little oil glands also store moisture in the form of oil in the leaves, useful in the dry Mediterranean climate where many herbs originated and where water would quickly evaporate.

It is these oils (also called *volatile oils* or *aromatic oils*) that give the plant its characteristic flavor and aroma. As it turns out, the better the growing conditions (good soil, plenty of nutrients, and adequate water), the more fully these little glands develop.

Because the oils are so volatile (they evaporate quickly and easily), most herbs, unlike spices, don't stand up well to prolonged cooking periods, and should best be added at the end of the cooking time.

How and why did people first begin to use herbs in their cooking? I can only guess that these flavorful green things made even the plainest ingredients taste more appealing.

Many years ago, I was working on a biography and staying in a small trailer near the creek that runs through Davis, California. The only cooking implements left behind by the former occupant were an old vintage 1970s Crock-Pot and a very unstable old frying pan.

In the spirit of adventure, I went to the local co-op and purchased every kind of bean it had, then cooked my way through them, taking just one kind of bean, cooking it, adding some good salt and then walking outside the kitchen to see what herbs were in the garden. I would usually flavor each soup with only one herb just to get a feeling for the purity of flavors in both the beans and the herb.

It may sound dull to some, but it was a wonderful experiment and led me to a career writing about the many things that can be done with a slow cooker—and now with herbs. Both are so practical and so useful for just about anything and everything.

I invite you to begin the adventure of getting to know the herbs in your garden (or out in nature) and to view any recipes as points of departure rather than as destinations in themselves. For this reason, I have chosen to present my recipes around a series of templates, or basic recipes that can become as different as night and day, depending upon how you choose to vary and arrange your ingredients. And I encourage you to play around with them and develop your own style and your own repertoire of recipes that work for you, your family, and your friends.

As with my book *50 Simple Soups for the Slow Cooker*, I have taken an "easy on the planet, the pocketbook, and the palate" approach because I believe many people today are looking for dishes that are easy to make, soul satisfying, and yet have a "conscience." I see no need for exotic ingredients, when in many cases, you can eat very well from your own backyard, supplemented by a few items from the farmers' market and supermarket.

There is no question that such a diet is relatively inexpensive (easy on the pocketbook), more healthful (does anyone still contest that a meat-based diet is not particularly healthful?), and a heck of a lot easier on the planet. In addition, growing some of our food, or even just the condiments, and spending some time with our feet planted in the soil every day, somehow begins to restore us to a closer connection with the land from which most of us have become so alienated.

A WORD ABOUT TABLEWARE

Digging around in the garden isn't the only way to maintain a closer connection with the earth. I've found a means of taking that feeling one step further. To wit, I delight in using plates, bowls, and cups made from the earth itself. I love the feel of handmade pottery in my hands, the resonance of a fork against the plate, or ice clinking in a stone or earthenware cup. There's a sense of soul in these handmade products: the soul of the earth, the soul of the potter, and the transformational magic of earth and fire—a heartbeat, if you will, that you will never find in a mass-produced, machine-made piece of work.

A WORD ABOUT THE RECIPES

I have enjoyed cooking with herbs out of my garden for many years, and the older I get, the more I appreciate simplicity in cooking, and in life in general. I no longer feel the need to rush around collecting exotic ingredients to feed myself, my family, and my friends. The challenge I have set myself today is to create something beautiful and enjoyable out of ingredients I have on hand or in the garden. I have no intention of giving up my Parmigiano-Reggiano, or a good Sonoma Dry Jack completely, but for the most part, I am happy with simple dishes.

When I was a little girl, I had a fashion-plate auntie. She was beautiful. She had charisma. She had great fashion sense. And she never stopped touting the merits of the classic "little black dress."

No matter what kind of budget you had, the little black dress should be the best you could possibly afford. Then, with a little ingenuity, you could dress it up or dress it down. Make a hundred outfits out of one simple black dress. And she did.

Auntie was no good in the kitchen. Her expertise was limited to the social register and the country club. But her "little black dress" theory works just as well in the kitchen as it did at the club or theater.

We should all have a few good template recipes—our culinary "little black dresses." There should be one each for our favorite dishes, and it should work every time. It should be simple enough to be whipped up fairly quickly. And it should not involve a lot of ingredients or exotic items. Above all, it should be flexible, so that with the addition of a little of this or some of that, it can go downtown or uptown, just like auntie's little black dress. In this case, variety can be supplied by an array of herbs and simple ingredients.

You will find a series of templates, or basic recipes, for each section in the book, with variations on a theme. In most cases, the first recipe in the section does not even include herbs in the ingredients. It is a blank slate, ripe for experiment. Use what you have. See what you like. By no means should you restrict yourself to the basic recipes or the variations. Be inspired by them to go out and create your own favorite recipes that you'll go back to again and again.

TIPS FOR COOKING WITH HERBS

- Wash herbs off in the garden, let them dry, then cut them.

- To dry larger quantities of herbs quickly, place them in a pillowcase and whirl it around. (You might want to go outside first, by the way.)

- Use a very clean, sharp knife for cutting herbs. You want to cut them cleanly, not mash or bruise them. Bruised herbs will oxidize and discolor quickly. If you are chopping them in a food processor, make sure the blade is good and sharp and that both the herbs and the processor are dry.

- To remove small-leafed herbs such as thyme or woody leaves such as rosemary, run your index finger and thumb down the stems.

- To chiffonade (cut into thin strips) herbs such as basil or mint, stack the leaves and roll them into a cigar shape, then, using a very sharp knife or a pair of sharp kitchen scissors, cut thin slices crosswise. A fresh herb chiffonade is a great finish for a dish.

- To snip small amounts of chives, gather the clean chives into a bundle, then snip them with very sharp scissors. It's a bit easier than using a knife.

- Consider allowing each herb to assert its own personality by choosing cooking and chopping techniques accordingly. Coarsely chopped herbs are good for more rustic dishes, and they yield their flavors more slowly to the finished dish. Finely chopped herbs are great for smoother dishes and will blend in with other ingredients very quickly, but they will also lose their flavors more quickly.

- Culinary herbs can loosely be divided into "sweet" and "resinous" categories:

  The sweet herbs are parsley, chervil, basil, cilantro, mint, hyssop, lovage, chives, tarragon, and dill. These always have more flavor when they are used fresh rather than dried.

  The resinous herbs are hardier, woodier, and more pungent (hence the name resin) than the sweet herbs. They tend to dry well, but are still generally best when used fresh. Savory, sage, marjoram, oregano, rosemary, and thyme fall into this category.

- Fresh herbs should generally be added to a dish at the last minute. Cooking or "standing around" quickly vaporizes the volatile oils that give herbs their flavor and aroma. If you chop and add them at the last minute, their textures remain evident and their flavors stand out. Dried or more resinous herbs can be added early on in the cooking process with greater success.

- Try using some whole herb leaves, such as basil, mint, cilantro, or parsley, in a green salad. My very favorite salad consists of nothing but parsley freshly picked from my garden, dressed with lemon juice, olive oil, and salt.

- At the height of the summer season, I love making bouquets of fresh herbs to place around the house as flower arrangements.

the herb
garden

As I began work on this book, it was November, and I found myself sitting by the fire and dreaming of springtime gardens and new life.

I'm always ambitious at this stage. Sitting in my favorite chair and dreaming of "work." I'm thinking of all the ways I can enrich the soil of my garden in preparation for planting. (You wouldn't bring home a new baby without getting all the stuff ready first, right?)

Preparing the soil is a year-round activity. In fact, fall and winter can be a great time for the soil to rest and be rejuvenated. I dig the pulp from my juicer right into the soil, where it should decompose by springtime, leaving plenty of organic matter and nutrients behind. And my local specialty coffee company bags up its spent coffee grounds daily for people like me to take home and work into the soil. There are oak trees not far away where I can simply take a bit of delicious oak mulch home in plastic trash bags to loosen the soil. And what about the stables at the local polo grounds? Just make sure that anything you put in your garden is free of pesticides or other chemicals.

Sourcing possible enrichments for the garden soil can be like a treasure hunt. It can be a lot of work, but a lot of fun, too. Although I love foraging for stuff to go into my garden, I don't always have the time for it, so Plan B consists of buying a good organic compost from the local nursery. I've recently found one that I like very much. It's a good, reliable source of humus for my soil, and that, coupled with my foraged organic matter, seems to be turning my rock-hard, sandstone backyard into a nice little jungle of edibles.

Some months ago, my friend Lorrie, who is of Native American descent, went with friends to attend a rain dance on one of the reservations not far from her home. Her e-mail account was fascinating, and because of that, I wanted to share it:

Traditionally the ceremony is meant to be viewed from the adobe rooftops, which are accessed by ladders . . . The Katsinas came up from the ground. Their feet moved in unison, creating a beat that sounded like hundreds of people clapping all at once. There was a loud droning sound created by their voices. There is no irrigation here, but each plot of land has a small patch of dirt with little rows of corn growing in it. The crops are grown only with rainwater and the people rely on praying for rain. I wish you could have been there with me to see the colors, hear the sounds, and remember the ways. This is a culture that has kept ancient traditions, ceremonies, secrets, and prophecies intact. As the last dance was ending and the early evening sun was pouring through the clouds in a heavenly manner, the wind started blowing hurricane hard. I looked down the alley into the plaza where the dancing took place, and a dust cloud had arisen that encircled the people better than any Hollywood film computer graphics could've done. It obscured my vision and clouded the pueblos and the people on top of the roofs . . . and then it started to rain.

Lorrie's story is touching and powerful and shows us how the Native American people acknowledged and worked with the forces of nature. I am told that ceremonies were used to draw the sunlight and the energy of the sun into the soil to help the young plants grow strong and to give them endurance.

I couldn't help wondering what would happen if, in addition to all the wonderful foraged treasures and organic fertilizers I apply to my garden, I, too, like our wise Native American friends, could say a quiet prayer to the forces of nature for some backup.

CHOOSING YOUR PLANTS

I address a few of the most popular culinary herbs in this book, but you needn't plant them all. Why not start with a few and see how it goes? Sit down and ask yourself whether some herbs in particular appeal to you. Which herbs would you really like to get to know? (If I were to answer that question right now, I'd probably choose dill, parsley, chives, and chervil. They are some of my favorites.)

Make your choices, then learn a bit about the herbs you've chosen before you plant them. For instance, how big will they get? Do they spread? Are they annuals (which need to be planted every year) or are they perennials (which last for several years)?

Most culinary herbs are Mediterranean in origin, which means that most of them like full sun. Herbs will grow in a variety of conditions; they just may not thrive. Herbs develop their best flavor when grown in full sunlight, with adequate nutrients and water. Their tempting flavors and aromas come as a result of volatile oils that develop in the plants as they grow. If you want to see what I mean, try an experiment. Buy some dill or basil from the grocery store, then do a comparison tasting with herbs grown outside in full sun. Almost without question, the herbs grown outdoors will be more flavorful and sturdy.

Coming from the Mediterranean region also means that most culinary herbs are fairly undemanding with regard to watering requirements. With adequate water, they will thrive. With insufficient water, they will be puny or may even die. In general, water them well when they dry out, but make sure you do not overwater them or leave them standing in water.

All herbs, with the possible exception of watercress, need well-drained soil, hence my emphasis on preparing your soil with plenty of organic matter before you plant your herbs. You want to encourage the growth of a strong root system, and the looser the soil, the easier it will be for your plants to send out roots and gather nutrients for themselves.

Herbs are essentially weeds, so most of them grow fairly easily, given basic beneficial conditions. As you may live in widely varying regions of the country, it seems a bit pointless to give instructions beyond the bare-bones basics. Herbs do as well in England as they do in southern Italy, for instance. You may simply have to alter your game plan from one locale to another.

ANNUAL OR PERENNIAL?

It's useful to know which herbs are going to be around for a while, and which herbs die off every year and need to be replenished. Annuals are plants that last only a year and must be replenished each year. Basil, chervil, cilantro, and dill are annuals. Perennials are plants that may last several years: chives, thyme, mint, marjoram, oregano, rosemary, sage, and tarragon are all perennials. Parsley is a biennial, meaning it produces its seeds in the second season of its life, then dies. It may be useful to place the annuals and the perennials together in different areas of the garden.

GROWING HERBS ORGANICALLY

Many people seem to be oblivious to the fact that farming is not an easy way of life. Most farmers are interested in one thing: maximizing their margins of profit. So for most conventional farmers, *your health is not the bottom line*. It is not that any of these hardworking people would deliberately poison you or your family, but in most cases, corporate farming operations and individual farmers will choose materials and methods that make their lives easier and their profits greater, and considerations of your health above and beyond what is legal are just not on the top of their checklist.

Consumers sometimes fool themselves into believing that only substances (including pesticides) that are not harmful are used on conventionally produced crops. But keep in mind that several months before I sat down to write this book, the California Department of Pesticide Regulations approved the use of a very potent *known carcinogen*, methyl iodide, for use in fumigating fields in California. They did this over the objections of a large number of very legitimate scientists and many consumer groups and individuals, clearly bowing to the economic pressures of agribusiness over the safety of farm workers and consumers. And this is only one of the more clear-cut cases of abuse.

You are the guardians of the health of your family, your pets, and your environment. And you cannot rely upon the government or agribusiness to put your welfare first.

In addition to the hazards posed to you and your family from synthetic pesticides, there are many dangers to your beloved pets. My vet, who has been in practice for nearly forty years, told me recently that when she first started to practice, cancer was seen only in older dogs and cats, but that now she sees it in animals who are only three or four years old. The connection between pesticide exposure and cancer in pets and humans is clear. So if you value your kitties and pups, don't place anything in your garden or soil that isn't clean and natural.

CONTAINER HERB GARDENING

Perhaps you have no garden in which to grow herbs, and you are thinking about putting a few pots on your terrace or back patio. Good idea. I nearly always have a few herbs around growing in pots, and I enjoy collecting pots in which my herbs look especially attractive. If you grow in pots, remember a few things: Start with good organic potting soil. (Again, that emphasis on organic. Just get out of the habit of buying chemical stuff. No one needs it, except the producers who are making money off it.) Be sure to pay attention and adjust both fertilizer and water appropriately. For instance, because they are porous, unglazed clay pots cause water to evaporate quickly, especially in hot weather; plastic pots may be unsightly, but they do a better job of conserving moisture. In most cases, let the soil in the pots just barely dry, then water again.

One day, a lady brought a handful of very sorry-looking basil to the herb farm. She asked me what was wrong. It had no flavor, poor color, and looked sick. I asked her whether the herbs were growing outside and she responded that they were growing outside in a pot. I asked how long they had been there and she told me she had been growing basil in the pot for several years! I asked if she had ever fertilized the poor things and her response was "No, I didn't know you needed to."

You must fertilize herbs in pots because they can't keep reaching out roots to new soil and nutrients. When you initially pot them in potting soil, there are nutrients in the soil that will help them grow. But fairly quickly those nutrients leach out through the bottom of the pot. Fertilize lightly every month or so during the growing season, using an organic fertilizer. Talk to your local nursery or garden center for suggested brands.

TIPS FOR GROWING HERBS

- Good soil is the key to successful gardening. Herbs need well-drained soil, so if you have a clay soil (where the water stands on the surface of the soil for more than a minute) add some good, organic compost, which adds nutrients and improves soil structure and permeability.

- They need adequate nutrients if they are to produce healthy leaves with full flavor, so be sure to provide some fertilizer and adequate water for them all the time. This is especially true if your herbs are planted in pots. All the plants in my garden (fruits, herbs, vegetables, roses) get a dose of good organic fertilizer when they are planted, and again two or three times during the growing season. Water your herbs as soon as the soil around them dries out.

- Most culinary herbs are Mediterranean in origin, which means they love the sun. Herbs grown in full sun will have a much stronger flavor than those grown indoors, in a hothouse, or even in the shade. Choose a spot where your plants will get at least six hours of direct sun each day.

- The flavor of the leaves begins to change once the plant has begun to flower, so it's important to keep the flowering heads of plants such as basil picked just as soon as they appear.

- If you are buying small starter plants from a nursery, or growing herbs from seed, do your homework. Find out how big/tall the mature plant might be so that you can plan your garden accordingly.

soups and
salads

Simple White Bean Soups: Simple Palate, So Many Variations

When I lived on a farm for several months while researching a book, I had nothing in the kitchen except a vintage 1970s Crock-Pot and an old frying pan. I went to the local health food coop and purchased as many different kinds of dried beans as I could find and experimented with making bean soup using nothing but beans, salt, and a couple of herbs from the small herb garden outside the kitchen door.

What I discovered was something that peasants the world over know: beans in and of themselves can make a delicious, satisfying meal. And each of them has its own unique flavor, texture, and color.

There is nothing quite so satisfying as a simple white bean soup. Laced with olive oil and some rosemary, it's one thing; drizzled with basil pesto, it's another. My Portuguese grandmother's people are famous for adding kale to everything, including white bean soup. Feel free to use your imagination and the ingredients you have on hand.

Basic White Bean Soup
Serves 6

I am very happy with this simple soup, and I eat it often. I recomm.
because that's the easiest and most effortless way to cook beans. The
depend upon the type of beans and how fresh they are. I also like to add
garlic at the end of the cooking time, for a fresher garlic flavor. And I cannot
the importance of adding enough salt to the soup. Without salt, the soup will t.
and uninteresting.

2 cups dried white beans (cannellini, navy, baby lima, whatever)

6 to 8 cups water (depending upon how thick you want the soup)

1 medium yellow onion, chopped

2 bay leaves

1 tablespoon salt, or more as desired

4 cloves garlic

Rinse the beans thoroughly and place them in the insert of a 6- or 7-quart slow cooker. Add the water, onion, and bay leaves and cook on high for about 4 hours or low for about 8 hours, or until the beans are tender.

When the beans are tender, add the salt and press the garlic into the soup. Remove and discard the bay leaves. Using a handheld immersion blender, puree some or all of the beans to thicken the soup. If you'd like a thinner consistency, add more water.

:an White Bean Soup with Olive Oil and Rosemary

es 6

ıngiafagioli. Bean eaters. That what they call 'em. Immortalized in a famous sixteenth-century painting housed in the Galleria Colonna in Rome, the painting celebrates centuries of what has kept the Tuscan peasant alive and well fed. I'm with 'em. Take a basic bean recipe, and doll it up with a few simple ingredients.

2 cups dried white beans (cannellini, navy, baby lima, whatever)

6 to 8 cups water (depending upon how thick you want the soup)

1 medium yellow onion, chopped

2 bay leaves

1 tablespoon salt, or more as desired

4 cloves garlic

¼ cup olive oil, for garnish

⅓ cup fresh rosemary leaves, chopped coarsely, for garnish

1 small, firm tomato, diced, for garnish

Rinse the beans thoroughly and place them in the insert of a 6- or 7-quart slow cooker. Add the water, onion, and bay leaves and cook on high for about 4 hours or low for about 8 hours, or until the beans are tender.

When the beans are tender, add the salt and press the garlic into the soup. Remove and discard the bay leaves. Using a handheld immersion blender, puree some or all of the beans to thicken the soup. If you'd like a thinner consistency, add more water.

Serve the soup in individual bowls, garnished with a generous drizzle of olive oil, a tablespoon of chopped, fresh rosemary, and a few pieces of tomato. Mangia tutti!

Soupe au Pistou
Serves 6

Nothing could be better than a pistou made with vegetables taken directly from your garden . . . or the farmers' market. The exact ingredients of this soup may vary from garden to garden and cook to cook, but it commonly contains zucchini, tomatoes, green beans, onion, and eggplant—all the favorite flavors of southern France. The unifying theme is the pistou, similar to Italian pesto: that earthy combination of lots of basil, olive oil, and Parmesan.

Soup

1 cup dried white beans (cannellini, navy, baby lima, whatever)

6 to 8 cups water (depending upon how thick you want the soup)

1 medium yellow onion, chopped

2 bay leaves

1 sprig fresh thyme

1 Parmesan rind (optional)

1 pound (about 4 medium) tomatoes, chopped

2 medium zucchini, diced

1 pound green beans, cut into 1-inch pieces

1 tablespoon salt, or more as desired

6 cloves garlic

continued

Pistou

2 cups tightly packed fresh basil leaves

½ cup freshly grated Parmesan cheese

3 large cloves garlic

¼ cup olive oil

Salt

Make the soup: Rinse the beans thoroughly and place them in the insert of a 6- or 7-quart slow cooker. Add the water, onion, bay leaves, thyme, and Parmesan rind, if using, and cook on HIGH for about 4 hours or LOW for about 8 hours, or until the beans are tender.

During the last hour of cooking, when the beans are almost tender, add the tomatoes, zucchini, and green beans and continue cooking until they are tender.

Add salt to taste and press the garlic into the soup. Remove and discard the bay leaves. You can use a handheld immersion blender to puree some or all of the beans to thicken the soup, if you wish.

Make the pistou: Place the basil, Parmesan, and garlic in the work bowl of a food processor and let the machine run until the basil and garlic are finely chopped. Turn off the machine, scrape down the sides of the bowl, then turn on the processor and drizzle the olive oil slowly through the feed tube until the pesto is smooth. Add salt to taste.

Ladle the soup into bowls, then drizzle some of the pistou into each bowl.

Portuguese White Bean Soup with Cilantro, Coriander, and Mint

Serves 6

My dear grandmother was not much of a cook, but she did have a few dishes inspired by her Portuguese ancestors, which she made often. Bean soup with kale, cilantro, and mint was one of them.

2 cups white beans (cannellini, navy, baby lima, whatever)

6 to 8 cups water (depending upon how thick you want the soup)

1 medium yellow onion, chopped

2 bay leaves

1 cup tomatoes, diced

2 cups kale, shredded

1 teaspoon coriander seeds, crushed

1 tablespoon salt, or more as desired

4 cloves garlic

⅓ cup coarsely chopped fresh cilantro leaves, for garnish

⅓ cup coarsely chopped fresh mint leaves, for garnish

Rinse the beans thoroughly and place them in the insert of a 6- or 7-quart slow cooker. Add the water, onion, and bay leaves and cook on HIGH for about 4 hours or LOW for about 8 hours, or until the beans are tender.

When the beans are almost tender, add the tomatoes, kale, and coriander seeds and continue cooking until the kale is wilted, about 20 minutes. Add salt to taste and press the garlic into the soup. Remove and discard the bay leaves.

Ladle the soup into bowls, then garnish with chopped cilantro and mint.

Salad Dressings: Greens on Greens

A good dressing can be used not only to lightly embellish garden fresh greens but also to drizzle over cooked vegetables, or as a dip for eating veggies raw and straight.

Buy good, organic oil in small amounts so that it is less likely to go rancid after sitting too long. This is especially important if you are using nut oils, because they are very fragile. Some of my favorite oils are organic extra-virgin olive oil, walnut oil, peanut oil, sesame seed oil (especially toasted), sunflower seed oil, and safflower oil. Store them in the refrigerator after they are opened. I also often buy unfiltered oils, which are cloudy, and which, to my mind, often have a deeper flavor than their filtered cousins.

I rarely use 100 percent olive oil in a salad dressing, as I find it over-whelming. I generally use a combination of a less distinctive oil, such as a filtered safflower or canola oil, in conjunction with a small portion of olive oil.

Proportions of vinegar or lemon juice to oil may vary greatly from recipe to recipe, but the basic formula of ¼ to ⅓ cup of vinegar or lemon juice to ⅔ to ¾ cup of oil seems to work in most cases.

You can use a mini food processor to blend the oils and chop the herbs, or you can do it the old-fashioned way, using a wire whisk. If I want a thicker dressing, I often drizzle in the oil slowly. Add garlic or not, as you like.

Basic Salad Dressing
Makes about 1 cup

The key to a good dressing is to use the best ingredients you can afford. I like using Meyer lemons from my tree, vinegar I have made in my own kitchen (or something else really interesting), and "designer" salt, for instance. Herbs, if used, always come straight out of the garden.

¼ to ⅓ cup vinegar or freshly squeezed lemon juice, or a combination

¼ to ½ teaspoon salt

1 clove garlic, pressed (optional)

1 teaspoon Dijon mustard (optional)

⅔ to ¾ cup extra-virgin olive oil or mixed oils

Freshly ground black pepper

Place the vinegar, salt, garlic, if using, and mustard, if using, in the work bowl of a mini food processor and blend well. With the processor running, slowly drizzle in the oil through the top. Add freshly ground black pepper to taste.

If you like doing things the old-fashioned way (and I often do), then start by placing the garlic and salt in a large mortar and pestle and smoosh them up. Then whisk in the vinegar and mustard. Slowly work in the oil while whisking, then grind in the pepper.

Basil Walnut Vinaigrette
Makes about 1 cup

Use this vinaigrette on a salad of fresh garden tomatoes and mozzarella, or drizzled over room temperature eggplant or green beans. It is also good with garden greens.

¼ cup wine vinegar, or half wine vinegar and half balsamic vinegar

1 tablespoon Dijon mustard

1 clove garlic, or more as desired

1 cup fresh basil leaves, chopped coarsely

¾ cup olive oil or mixed oils

Salt and freshly ground black pepper

½ cup walnuts, chopped coarsely and toasted

Combine the vinegar, mustard, garlic, and basil in the work bowl of a food processor and process for 1 minute. Scrape down the sides of the bowl, then with the motor running, slowly drizzle in the olive oil.

Add salt and pepper to taste, then add the walnuts, pulsing only until the walnut pieces have reached the desire texture. Do not pulverize them.

Cilantro-Coriander Vinaigrette

Makes about 1 cup

For some reason, the seeds of the cilantro plant are most commonly referred to as coriander seeds, whereas the leaves are most commonly termed cilantro. This recipe contains both the seeds and the leaves, and would be great drizzled over a sliced avocado and grapefruit salad.

2 cloves garlic, pressed

⅓ cup vinegar, or 3 tablespoons freshly squeezed lemon or lime juice plus 3 tablespoons vinegar

⅔ cup olive oil or mixed oils

2 teaspoons coriander seeds, toasted

½ cup fresh cilantro leaves

½ teaspoon salt

Freshly ground black pepper

Combine the garlic and vinegar in the work bowl of a mini food processor and blend well. Scrape down the sides of the bowl, then with the processor running, slowly drizzle in the oil.

Add the coriander seeds, cilantro, salt, and pepper to taste, then pulse until the dressing reaches your desired consistency.

Rice Salad: A Meal in Itself

Although Americans rarely eat warm or cold rice salads or rice as an entrée, I was surprised to find a warm rice salad on the entrée menu at the lovely Inn of the Seventh Ray in Topanga Canyon, just north of Los Angeles. It was delicious and set me thinking about the possibilities of rice and rice salads as the basis for a meal.

Basic Brown Rice
Serves 2 to 4, depending upon how hungry you are

Most of us probably use a rice cooker to cook rice. It's convenient and easy, but may not always produce a light, fluffy finished product. If you're in a hurry, go ahead and use the rice cooker. I do. But if you've got a little more time, and you'd like a nice, light, fluffy batch of rice as a basis for a salad, why not try cooking it the old-fashioned way: boiled in a pot with lots of water, just as you would cook pasta. You can prepare your favorite toppings while the rice cooks.

4 quarts water

1 tablespoon salt

2 cups uncooked long-grain brown rice, rinsed

Bring the water and salt to a boil in a large pot over medium-high heat.

Add the rice and boil briskly until the grains are al dente, about 40 minutes. The cooking time may vary accordingly with the variety of rice.

When the rice is al dente, drain it in a colander, rinse lightly under cool water, then drain thoroughly.

Put the rice in a wide bowl and fluff it up with your fingers. It's ready to serve with your favorite toppings, or to use in a salad.

Greek-Style Rice Salad with Dill Dressing
Serves 4 to 6

If you let this salad sit for a few hours after preparing it, whether at room temperature or in the refrigerator, the flavors begin to blend and deepen. In short, the whole is greater than the sum of its parts. My friend Kathy thinks this is the best thing that ever came out of my kitchen.

1 recipe Basic Brown Rice (page 21)

1 medium cucumber, peeled and diced finely

2 medium tomatoes, diced finely

1 cup Mediterranean black olives, sliced in half and pitted

1 green bell pepper, seeded and diced finely

1 (7-ounce) package feta cheese, crumbled

Vinaigrette

3 cloves garlic, pressed

3 tablespoons freshly squeezed lemon juice

3 tablespoons vinegar

⅔ cup olive oil or mixed oils

2 teaspoons dill seeds

¼ cup chopped fresh dill leaves

1 teaspoon salt

Freshly ground black pepper

continued

In a large bowl, combine the rice, cucumber, tomatoes, olives, green pepper, and feta.

Make the vinaigrette: Combine the garlic, lemon juice, and vinegar in the work bowl of a mini food processor and blend well. Scrape down the sides of the bowl, then with the processor running, slowly drizzle in the oil. Add the dill seeds, dill leaves, salt, and pepper to taste, then pulse until the dressing reaches your desired consistency.

Toss the vinaigrette with the salad. Refrigerate for at least an hour or two before serving. Serve chilled, or let the salad come to room temperature first.

Tabbouleh-Style Rice Salad with Tomatoes, Cucumber, and Parsley-Mint Vinaigrette

Serves 4 to 6

Like the Greek-Style Rice Salad with Dill Dressing (page 23), this can be served at room temperature or cold, over a few leaves of romaine lettuce.

1 recipe Basic Brown Rice (page 21)

2 cups finely diced tomatoes

1 medium cucumber, peeled and diced finely

½ cup thinly sliced scallions

Vinaigrette

⅔ cup olive oil or mixed oils

3 tablespoons freshly squeezed lemon juice

3 tablespoons vinegar

2 tablespoons fresh parsley leaves

2 tablespoons fresh mint leaves

1 teaspoon salt

2 pinches of ground cinnamon

Freshly ground black pepper

½ head romaine lettuce, torn into bite-size pieces

continued

In a large bowl, combine the rice, tomatoes, cucumber, and scallions.

Combine all of the vinaigrette ingredients in the work bowl of a food processor and pulse until the herbs are finely chopped and everything is thoroughly mixed.

Toss the vinaigrette with the salad. Refrigerate for at least an hour or two before serving. Serve chilled on a bed of romaine lettuce, or let the salad come to room temperature first.

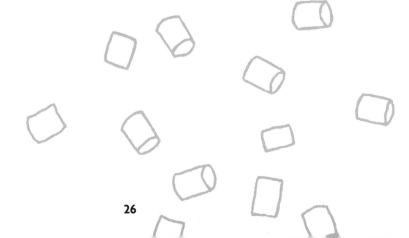

Brown Rice, Olive, and Artichoke Salad with Chive and Oregano Vinaigrette
Serves 4 to 6

This is a delightful, light, healthful, flavorful rice salad. The olives give it a touch of salt, and you can use artichokes, peas, or broccoli, all with equally good results. The dressing is light and lemony, and for an even lighter touch, I have substituted tomato juice from my garden tomatoes for half of the oil. You can serve the rice on a bed of lettuce and add cooked white or black beans for extra protein, then serve either plain or nestled in a leaf or two of butter lettuce.

1 recipe Basic Brown Rice (page 21), warm or cold

1 cup black Mediterranean-style olives, halved

1 cup artichoke hearts, sliced (see Note)

Vinaigrette

4 tablespoons freshly squeezed lemon juice

1 large egg

⅔ cup olive oil or mixed oils

4 cloves garlic, peeled

¼ cup chopped fresh chives

¼ cup chopped fresh oregano leaves

1 teaspoon salt, or more as desired

Freshly ground black pepper

continued

In a large bowl, combine the rice, olives, and artichokes. Set aside.

Place the lemon juice and egg in the work bowl of a mini food processor and blend until frothy. With the processor running, slowly drizzle in the olive oil from the top. Press the garlic into the dressing. Add the chives and oregano, then add salt and pepper to taste and thoroughly blend everything together.

Toss the vinaigrette with the salad. Serve warm or at room temperature.

Note: I prefer fresh baby artichoke hearts, but canned or frozen will work.

main
dishes

Polenta: Three Ways to Breakfast, Lunch, or Dinner

A simple plate of polenta (ground dried corn) can serve as a meal in itself. It may be topped with some butter and a dusting of freshly grated Parmesan, or it can be topped with something a little more filling and elaborate, such as marinara sauce, steamed veggies, a fried egg, or roasted chiles, to name a few. You can serve polenta in a bowl as a meal, or in appetizer portions on small plates or in small bowls.

Basic Polenta

Serves 4 to 6

The classic method of making polenta would have you stirring it in a saucepan over medium heat until it thickens and pulls away from the sides of the pot, but it requires very little stirring to turn out a batch of decent polenta in a slow cooker. Cook the polenta on high while you prepare the rest of your meal or cook on low overnight for a great, hearty breakfast.

5 cups water

1 cup polenta

1 teaspoon salt

Combine all the ingredients in a 4-quart slow cooker. Cover and cook on low for about 6 hours or on high for about 1½ hours, stirring a few times, until the polenta is creamy and the grains are tender.

Polenta with Marinara, Ricotta Cheese, and Basil

Serves 4

Polenta can be served as a side to something more substantial, but Italians often eat it as a meal or a course in itself.

1 recipe Basic Polenta (page 31)

1 cup marinara sauce, heated

1 cup ricotta cheese

½ cup freshly grated Parmesan cheese

1 cup fresh basil leaves, cut in chiffonade (see Note)

Either spoon the prepared polenta into a large serving bowl or mound scoops of it on four individual plates or in individual bowls. Top with hot marinara sauce, then add a scoop of ricotta and a dusting of Parmesan.

Garnish with a shower of basil leaves and serve immediately.

Note: To chiffonade (cut in thin strips) the basil, stack the clean, dry leaves, then roll them into a cigar shape and using a very sharp knife, slice them crosswise.

Southwestern Grits with Tomatoes, Queso Fresco, Onion, Olives, Cilantro, Avocado, and Lime

Serves 4

Polenta is a cousin to grits, and here it is served with a Southwestern flair. I would eat this for breakfast, lunch, or dinner and not think twice about it. It is sort of like a taco in a bowl.

1 recipe Basic Polenta (page 31)

2 medium tomatoes, diced

1 cup queso fresco or feta cheese, crumbled

½ medium white onion, chopped

½ cup sliced black olives

½ cup diced avocado

½ cup coarsely chopped fresh cilantro leaves

1 lime, cut into wedges

Spoon the prepared polenta into one large serving bowl or four individual bowls. Top with the tomatoes, queso fresco, onion, olives, avocado, and cilantro.

Serve immediately with individual wedges of lime for squeezing.

Grits with Smoked Gouda, Sharp Cheddar, Onions, Chives, and Parsley

Serves 4

You might say that grits are the Southerner's polenta, and you wouldn't be far wrong. Grits are most commonly served for breakfast in the South, sweetened with sugar or laced with cheese or country sausage. I love the smokehouse flavor added by a good smoked Gouda cheese. If you're feeling lazy, leave out the onion altogether and just go for a cheese fest.

1 tablespoon unsalted butter or oil

½ medium yellow onion, sliced thinly

1 cup grated smoked Cheddar or Gouda cheese

¼ cup chopped fresh chives

1 recipe Basic Polenta, still hot (page 31)

½ cup chopped fresh parsley

½ cup grated sharp Cheddar

Melt the butter in a large sauté pan over medium-high heat. Add the onion and cook until golden brown, about 10 minutes.

Stir the smoked Cheddar and chives into the hot polenta. Spoon the polenta into one large serving bowl or four individual bowls. Top with the sautéed onion, parsley, and sharp Cheddar and serve immediately.

Potatoes Rösti: Breakfast, Lunch, or Dinner

My grandfather grew up on a ranch in the Sierras. Potatoes and eggs fried in bacon grease offered him and his brothers the means to do a hard day's work, and he always made hash browns for me when he would come to visit. To this day, fried potatoes are still one of my favorite breakfasts. I just don't fry them in bacon grease anymore.

We Americans love our hash browns, but potatoes have been a breakfast staple for people around the western world for centuries. *Rösti*, or *roesti*, is the name for a popular Swiss breakfast that is nothing more and nothing less than a plate full o' hash browns. Believed to have originated as a farmer's breakfast in the Swiss canton of Bern, its popularity spread rapidly and today it can be found throughout Switzerland for breakfast, lunch, or dinner.

A *rösti* seasoned with nothing but salt and pepper is great, but being this is a book about herbs, I'm focusing on some herb variations.

Finally, buying organic potatoes seems especially important to me as nearly all conventionally grown potatoes found in stores today are (1) genetically modified and (2) loaded with fungicides and pesticides. Do yourself a favor and buy only organic.

Basic Rösti
Serves 2 to 4

If you don't own a cast-iron skillet, may I suggest you get one? Cast iron is inexpensive and invaluable, especially for making a dish like this one. Nothing gives quite the golden brown crust that a well-seasoned cast-iron skillet can do. Today, you can even buy cast-iron skillets that have been preseasoned at almost any kitchenware shop or hardware store. I use a 10 ½-inch cast-iron skillet for making a large *rösti*, or an 8-inch one for making individual-size *rösti*. Certainly, you can make the *rösti* in a regular sauté pan or skillet, but cast iron is hard to beat.

2 tablespoons olive oil

2 large organic russet potatoes, grated

Salt

Freshly ground black pepper

Place the olive oil in a large skillet over medium heat and allow the skillet to heat thoroughly, 3 to 4 minutes. It's important not to get the skillet too hot, as the potatoes on the bottom will cook before the insides are done.

Squeeze as much liquid as possible out of the grated potatoes, then place them in a bowl and toss them with salt and pepper.

Place the grated potatoes in the skillet and press them down with a spatula into an even layer. Cook for about 10 minutes, rotating the skillet a couple of times to avoid hot spots, until the bottom of the *rösti* is golden brown. You can lift the *rösti* with a spatula to peek.

Loosen the *rösti* on the sides and bottom of the pan with a spatula, slide the *rösti* out onto a plate, then slide the *rösti* back into the pan, browned side up. Cook for another 10 minutes, until the underside of the *rösti* is also browned.

Gently run a spatula around the sides of and underneath the *rösti* and slide it onto your serving plate. Serve immediately.

Garnet Yam Rösti with Indian Flavors

Serves 4

While I love good old russets, I also love bright orangey-red yams and thought that they would make just as good a *rösti* as the russets. And think of the color! The only thing is, grated yams are a bit drier than grated russets, so you'll want an egg white or two to help bind them together.

2 tablespoons ghee (clarified butter) or vegetable oil

4 large red or garnet yams

1 teaspoon salt

Freshly ground black pepper

2 teaspoons coriander seeds, crushed

2 teaspoons cumin seeds, crushed

2 egg whites

½ cup plain yogurt

½ cup coarsely chopped fresh cilantro

½ cup thinly sliced scallions

½ serrano chile, chopped finely

Place the ghee in a large skillet over medium heat and allow the skillet to heat thoroughly, 3 to 4 minutes. It's important not to get the skillet too hot, as the potatoes on the bottom will cook before the insides are done.

Place the yams in a large bowl and toss them with salt, pepper, coriander and cumin seeds, and egg whites.

continued

Place the yams in the skillet and press them down with a spatula into an even layer. Cook for about 10 minutes, rotating the skillet a couple of times to avoid hot spots, until the bottom of the *rösti* is golden brown.

Loosen the *rösti* on the sides and bottom of the pan with a spatula, slide the *rösti* out onto a plate, then slide the *rösti* back into the pan, browned side up. Cook for another 10 minutes, or until the underside of the *rösti* is also browned.

Gently run a spatula around the sides of and underneath the rösti and slide it onto your serving plate. Top with the yogurt, cilantro, scallions, and chile and serve immediately.

Irish Potatoes with Cheddar, Chives, Parsley, and Sour Cream

Serves 2 to 4

Even though they let the Irish workingman down, potatoes remain today one of the favorite foods of the Irish, and little wonder. Potatoes are filling, can be dolled up in myriad ways, combine well with the wonderful Irish dairy products, and sustain life. Irish cookbooks are filled with many different ways to prepare and serve potatoes. Here is one of my favorites.

2 tablespoons oil

2 large organic russet potatoes, grated

1 teaspoon salt

Freshly ground black pepper

¼ cup finely chopped fresh chives

½ cup finely chopped yellow onion

¼ cup sour cream

¼ cup Irish Cheddar cheese, grated

2 tablespoons fresh parsley, chopped

Place the oil in a large skillet over medium heat and allow the skillet to heat thoroughly, 3 to 4 minutes. It's important not to get the skillet too hot, as the potatoes on the bottom will cook before the insides are done.

Squeeze as much liquid as possible out of the grated potatoes, then place them in a large bowl and toss them with salt and pepper. Add the chives and onion and toss to mix.

Place the potatoes in the skillet and press them with a spatula into an even layer. Cook for about 10 minutes, rotating the skillet a couple of times to avoid hot spots, until the bottom of the *rösti* is golden brown.

Loosen the *rösti* on the sides and bottom of the pan with a spatula, slide the *rösti* out onto a plate, then slide the *rösti* back into the pan, browned side up. Cook for another 10 minutes, until the underside of the *rösti* is also browned.

Gently run a spatula around the sides of and underneath the *rösti* and slide it onto your serving plate. Top with the sour cream, Cheddar, and parsley and serve immediately.

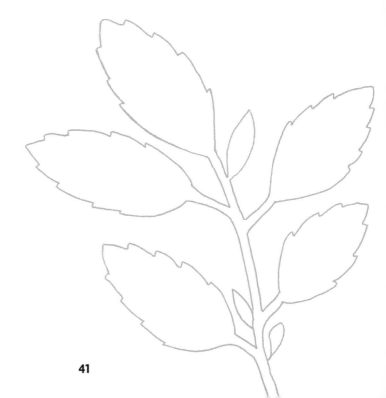

Potato, Olive, and Rosemary Rösti
Serves 2 to 4

Perhaps one of the world's best combinations is that of rosemary and potatoes. Roasted freshly dug potatoes sprinkled with some olive oil, rosemary, and salt are spectacular. And a rösti featuring nothing but potato, olives, and rosemary is just as good.

2 tablespoons olive oil

2 large organic russet potatoes, grated

Salt

Freshly ground black pepper

¼ cup rosemary, chopped coarsely

½ cup black Mediterranean-style olives, quartered

½ cup freshly grated Parmesan cheese

Place the olive oil in a large skillet over medium heat and allow the skillet to heat thoroughly, 3 to 4 minutes. It's important not to get the skillet too hot, as the potatoes on the bottom will cook before the insides are done.

Squeeze as much liquid as possible out of the grated potatoes, then place them in a large bowl and toss them with salt and pepper. Add the rosemary and olives and toss to mix.

Place the mixture in the skillet and press them down with a spatula into an even layer. Cook for about 10 minutes, rotating the skillet a couple of times to avoid hot spots, until the bottom of the *rösti* is golden brown.

Loosen the *rösti* on the sides and bottom of the pan with a spatula, slide the *rösti* out onto a plate, then slide the *rösti* back into the pan, browned side up. Cook for another 10 minutes, until the underside of the *rösti* is also browned.

Gently run a spatula around the sides of and underneath the *rösti* and slide it onto your serving plate. Top with the Parmesan and serve immediately.

Fresh Herb Pasta: Herbs in the Dough or on Top

Making pasta by hand is fun and easy. It just takes some time, especially when you are first learning, but it's well worth the effort, as everyone loves freshly made pasta.

I like to set aside a morning or afternoon for making pasta. The only tricky part is rolling the dough thinly enough. You can easily do this using a hand-cranked Italian pasta machine, or you can roll it out by hand with a rolling pin. In either case, you want to make sure that you can see the shadow of your hand through the pasta when you hold it up to the light.

Basic Pasta
Makes 1 pound, which serves 4 to 6

You can incorporate fresh herbs into the pasta dough for a subtle touch and a nice visual effect. Or you can make it plain and top it with plenty of herbs, butter, and olive oil. I thought I'd give a simple fresh pasta recipe and let you make the call as to whether you want to incorporate the herbs in the pasta itself or use them in a sauce.

2 cups unbleached bread flour, plus more for dusting

2 large eggs

½ teaspoon salt

1 tablespoon olive oil

¼ cup chopped fresh herbs (optional)

3 to 4 tablespoons water

Place the flour, eggs, salt, and olive oil in the work bowl of a food processor and pulse until the mixture looks like cornmeal. If you are adding fresh herbs, now would be the time to add them.

Add 3 tablespoons of water and pulse again briefly. Then let the machine run until the dough forms a clean ball in the processor, about 45 seconds. If the dough doesn't come together smoothly and easily, add more water, 1 teaspoon at a time.

Remove the ball of dough from the processor. Roll it in plastic wrap into a 6-inch cylinder, then let it rest for at least 1 hour at room temperature. The dough will relax while it sits, making it easier to work with.

To roll out the dough, you can use a stainless-steel roller-type pasta machine and run the dough through the machine according to the manufacturer's instructions. If you do not

continued

have a pasta machine, cut the cylinder into six pieces. Have some flour on hand to keep the pasta sheets from sticking to the board as you work. Use a rolling pin to roll out each piece of dough on a lightly floured surface into a rectangle about 12 inches in length, and then fold it over into three layers. Cut the dough into strips. Shape the pasta strips out, then place them on a baking sheet to begin drying out. You can also use the old Italian housewife's trick: Prop a clean stick or broom handle between the backs of two chairs, then hang the strands of pasta over it.

To cook the pasta: Bring a large pot of salted water to a boil. Add the pasta and cook until al dente, about 3 minutes. Drain, sauce, and serve.

Herb and Garlic Pasta

Serves 4 to 6

Once you've perfected plain pasta, you can dress it up with garlic, olive oil, Parmesan cheese, and herbs fresh from the garden.

4 cloves garlic

½ cup freshly grated Parmesan

½ cup grated Cheddar or fontina cheese (optional)

⅓ cup extra-virgin olive oil

2 tablespoons coarsely chopped fresh parsley

2 tablespoons coarsely chopped fresh sage

2 tablespoons coarsely chopped fresh basil

Salt

2 firm tomatoes, diced

1 recipe Basic Pasta (page 45), cooked and drained

Place the garlic, Parmesan, Cheddar, if using, olive oil, and herbs in the work bowl of a food processor and pulse until the mixture forms the texture of coarse cornmeal. (If you'd like the herbs to be in more recognizable pieces, set them aside and chop coarsely with a knife, then toss them in with the pasta and the other ingredients.) Add salt to taste.

Toss the cheese mixture and the tomatoes with the pasta and serve immediately.

Pasta with Crème Fraîche and Gremolata
Serves 4 to 6

Gremolata is the traditional Italian blend of garlic, parsley, and lemon zest. Saucing pasta with something as simple as crème fraîche or sour cream and *gremolata* is another easy way to use the bounty of the herb garden and keep everybody happy at the same time.

Gremolata

4 cloves garlic

½ cup coarsely chopped fresh parsley

3 heaping tablespoons fresh lemon zest

1 recipe Basic Pasta (page 45), cooked and drained

1 cup crème fraîche or sour cream, warmed

⅓ cup freshly grated Parmesan cheese

Salt

Make the gremolata: Finely chop together the garlic, parsley, and lemon zest. Set aside.

In a large bowl, quickly toss the pasta with the crème fraîche, Parmesan, and *gremolata*. Add plenty of salt, then serve immediately.

Herbed Pasta Alfredo
Serves 4 to 6

One of my favorite dishes is also one of the most simple: pasta Alfredo. This is a variation using basil and peas for a little additional interest.

1 cup heavy cream

4 tablespoons (½ stick) butter

2 cups freshly grated Parmesan cheese

1 recipe Basic Pasta (page 45), cooked and drained

1 cup fresh peas

Salt

Freshly ground black pepper

½ cup fresh basil, cut in chiffonade (see Note, page 32)

Place the cream and butter in a large saucepan and bring to a simmer over medium heat. Add half the Parmesan, whisk until smooth, and remove from the heat.

Add the pasta and peas and toss to mix. Add plenty of salt and pepper. Serve immediately with the remaining Parmesan and the basil sprinkled over the top.

Pasta with Tarragon and Walnuts
Serves 4 to 6

Tarragon is more commonly considered a part of the French culinary repertoire, but the herb can sometimes also be found in northern Italian cooking. Make a delicious, simple pasta dish using tarragon or any favorite fresh herb in the spring when the herbs are tender and flavorful.

2 tablespoons olive oil

2 tablespoons unsalted butter

2 cloves garlic

1 recipe Basic Pasta (page 45), cooked and drained

2 tablespoons coarsely chopped fresh tarragon

2 tablespoons chopped fresh parsley

Salt

Freshly ground black pepper

½ cup freshly grated Parmesan cheese

⅓ cup walnuts, toasted and chopped coarsely

Warm the oil and butter in a small pan, then press the garlic into the pan.

Add the pasta, tarragon, and parsley and toss to mix. Add salt and pepper to taste. Top with the Parmesan and walnuts and serve.

Mac 'n' Cheese: Comfort Classic with a Twist

In my book, the quality of the mac 'n' cheese is a good yardstick against which to measure any restaurant. It was the first thing I ever learned how to make, and it's often the first thing I'll choose from a restaurant menu if I have reason to believe it'll be good. There are so many possible variations and so many potential add-ins: cooked vegetables such as broccoli, cauliflower, bell peppers, carrots, kale, or even Brussels sprouts; and, of course, herbs fresh from the garden. Each one can lend a new face to an old favorite.

Basic Mac 'n' Cheese

Serves 4

Here is a basic mac 'n' cheese recipe, followed by two possible herb-and-cheese variations. The recipe produces a very generous serving of cheese sauce. If you prefer a little less, use 3 ½ cups of milk rather than 4.

4 tablespoons (½ stick) unsalted butter (see Note)

¼ cup all-purpose flour

3 ½ cups whole milk

4 cups grated cheese

Salt

½ pound pasta, cooked al dente and drained

Optional add-ins: fresh herbs, peas, broccoli, carrots, tomatoes

Preheat the oven to 350°F and place a rack in the center.

Melt the butter in a large saucepan over medium heat, then whisk in the flour and continue to cook for about 2 minutes more, just until the flour and butter froth.

Slowly add the milk, whisking constantly. The "slowly" part is important because it will allow the sauce to thicken to the consistency of a very heavy cream. When the sauce coats the back of a spoon thickly, remove the saucepan from the heat and add 3 cups of the cheese, whisking until it has been incorporated into the sauce. Whisk in some salt.

In a large bowl, pour the sauce over the cooked pasta, then stir in any add-ins. Taste and adjust the salt if necessary.

Spoon the mixture into a 9 by 13-inch baking dish. At this point, you can cover and refrigerate overnight if you wish. Top with the reserved cup of cheese and bake for about 20 minutes, or until hot and the cheese topping is melted and turning golden.

If you refrigerated the casserole, you will need to heat it thoroughly, which may take 30 to 40 minutes.

Let rest for about 15 minutes before serving.

Note: For a lower-fat version of the sauce, I leave out the butter entirely and froth the flour and milk in a blender, pour it into a saucepan, and bring it to a simmer, whisking constantly until it becomes the consistency of heavy cream. It's not a bad substitution at all.

Mediterranean Olive, Sun-Dried Tomato, and Oregano Mac
Serves 4

There are Mediterranean flavors in this classic American dish. While the cheeses can be varied, I love the salty, tangy flavor of feta and often leave a few small chunks of it in the sauce for added texture.

4 tablespoons (½ stick) unsalted butter

¼ cup all-purpose flour

3 ½ cups whole milk

8 ounces feta cheese, crumbled

1 cup grated fontina or Monterey Jack cheese

Salt

½ pound pasta, cooked al dente and drained

½ cup Mediterranean-style olives (black or green), halved

½ cup sun-dried tomatoes, sliced, or 1 cup canned diced tomatoes, well drained

⅓ cup coarsely chopped fresh Greek oregano leaves

2 tablespoons chopped fresh rosemary leaves

Preheat the oven to 350°F and place a rack in the center.

Melt the butter in a large saucepan over medium heat, then whisk in the flour and continue to cook for about 2 minutes more, just until the flour and butter froth.

Slowly add the milk, whisking constantly. The "slowly" part is important because it allows the sauce to thicken to the consistency of a very heavy cream. When the sauce coats the back of a spoon thickly, remove the saucepan from the heat and add the cheeses, whisking until they have been incorporated into the sauce. I like to leave a few small chunks of feta. Whisk in some salt.

In a large bowl, pour the sauce over the cooked pasta, then stir in the olives, tomatoes, oregano, and rosemary. Taste and adjust the salt if necessary.

Spoon the mixture into a 9 by 13-inch baking dish. At this point, you can refrigerate the casserole overnight if you wish. Bake for about 20 minutes, or until heated throughout. If you refrigerated the casserole, you will need to heat it thoroughly, which may take 30 to 40 minutes.

Let rest for about 15 minutes before serving.

Blue Cheese, Artichoke Heart, and Tarragon Mac
Serves 4

The combination of blue cheese and pasta can be found in northern Italy, often topped with a sprinkle of chopped walnuts. Use Italian Gorgonzola (produced mainly in the Piedmont and Lombardy) or domestic blue cheese. Either way, you'll love the rich, creamy finished product, accented by the slightly aniselike flavors of artichoke and tarragon that complement each other so well.

4 tablespoons (½ stick) unsalted butter

¼ cup all-purpose flour

3 ½ cups whole milk

8 ounces blue cheese, crumbled

4 ounces goat cheese

Salt

½ pound pasta, cooked al dente and drained

12 ounces frozen artichoke hearts, thawed

¼ cup coarsely chopped fresh tarragon leaves

½ cup walnuts, chopped coarsely

Preheat the oven to 350°F and place a rack in the center.

Melt the butter in a large saucepan over medium heat, then whisk in the flour and continue to cook for about 2 minutes more, just until the flour and butter froth.

Slowly add the milk, whisking constantly. The "slowly" part is important because it will allow the sauce to thicken to the consistency of a very heavy cream. When the sauce coats the back of a spoon thickly, remove the saucepan from the heat and add the cheeses, whisking until they have been incorporated into the sauce. Whisk in some salt.

In a large bowl, pour the sauce over the cooked pasta, then stir in the artichoke hearts and tarragon. Taste and adjust the salt if necessary.

Spoon the mixture into a 9 by 13-inch baking dish, sprinkle the walnuts on top, and bake for about 20 minutes, until heated through.

Let sit for about 15 minutes before serving.

Pizza: Fresh Herbs on a Favorite Dish

I've eaten pizzas all over the world, yet the pizzas I like best are the ones I make at home, baked on my own pizza stone, and topped with tomatoes from my garden and a judicious sprinkling of my favorite cheeses and freshly picked herbs.

Pizza was the original fast food of the Mediterranean world, the sandwich of ancient peoples. The Romans ate something that translated to "bread with a relish" for breakfast, and the remains of something that looked like pizza have been found in the ruins at Pompeii.

The possibilities for interesting pizza toppings are limitless. They range from simple breads topped with some good olive oil, freshly picked herbs, and a sprinkling of Parmesan, to those with more elaborate sauces and ingredients. As always, I encourage experimentation, using the recipes here as a template. Note: I nearly always sprinkle fresh herbs over a pizza only **after** the pizza comes out of the oven, to preserve a bright look and fresh flavor.

Basic Pizza

Serves 4

There is something very satisfying about watching a simple lump of dough sauced with tomatoes, herbs, and cheese puff up in the oven and come out steaming hot and fragrant. I've made
it hundreds of times and each time, using whatever is in the kitchen, garden, or cupboard, and
rarely have I been disappointed. Make the dough plain or lace it with olives and herbs.

3 cups flour, preferably freshly milled whole wheat, plus more for rolling

2 teaspoons SAF instant yeast

1 teaspoon salt

2 tablespoons olive oil, plus more for coating

1 cup water, plus more if needed

Your favorite sauce, toppings and cheese

Combine the flour, yeast, and salt in the work bowl of a food processor and pulse to mix.

Add the olive oil to the water, then with the machine running, quickly pour the liquid
down the feed tube and let the machine run until the dough forms a clean ball in the food
processor. This should take no more than a minute or two.

Remove the dough ball from the food processor and pat it into a flat, round disk. Place
a thin coating of oil on the outside of the dough and put it in a large plastic bag. At this
point, you can press the air out of the bag, then freeze the dough for later use. Let it rest
for 20 to 30 minutes. (If you are freezing the dough, remove it from the freezer a few hours
before you plan to bake, then let it come to room temperature before rising.)

Preheat the oven to 500°F about 15 minutes before baking. This ensures a nice, hot oven
that will give your pizza a beautiful, light, crispy crust.

continued

Assemble your pizza toppings while the dough rests. Make sure to choose ingredients that are as dry as possible—excess moisture will make your pizza soggy. Also remember that "Less is more" applies equally well to life, fashion, and pizza making.

With a rolling pin, roll the dough out into a fairly thin circle or rectangle, on a lightly floured surface.

Lay the dough on a baking sheet covered with parchment paper or a silicone baking mat with a light dusting of cornmeal. (If you're a pizza aficionado, you can use a pizza peel dusted with cornmeal, and a baking stone.) Let the dough rest for about 15 minutes.

Add your sauce, toppings, and cheese, then bake for about 10 minutes, or until the crust looks golden, the cheese is melted, and the toppings are cooked.

Mexican-Style Pizza with Green Chile Sauce, Cilantro, and Mexican Oregano

Serves 4

You can use a homemade, thickened green chile or tomatillo sauce, but if you're in a hurry, you can easily used a canned green chile enchilada sauce. Or if you're a dedicated Mexican cook, you can even use a homemade mole sauce for your base. Add the herbs only after the pizza has come out of the oven, to retain their fresh flavor.

1 recipe Basic Pizza dough (page 59)

1 cup thick green chile sauce or tomatillo sauce

½ teaspoon coarsely ground coriander seeds

½ teaspoon coarsely ground cumin seeds

1 firm tomato, sliced thinly

½ cup crumbled queso fresco, smoked Gouda, or feta cheese, or a combination

¼ cup sliced black olives, well drained

2 scallions, green parts only, sliced thinly

2 teaspoons Mexican oregano (see Note)

2 tablespoons coarsely chopped fresh cilantro leaves

1 tablespoon chopped fresh parsley

Preheat the oven to 500°F about 15 minutes before baking.

With a rolling pin, roll the dough out into a fairly thin circle or rectangle, on a lightly floured surface.

continued

Lay the dough on a baking sheet covered with parchment paper or a silicone baking mat with a light dusting of cornmeal. (If you're a pizza aficionado, you can use a pizza peel dusted with cornmeal, and a baking stone.) Let the dough rest for about 15 minutes.

Sauce the dough lightly, then evenly distribute all the other ingredients except the cilantro and parsley. Bake for about 10 minutes, or until the crust looks golden, the cheese is melted, and the toppings are cooked.

Remove from the oven, sprinkle the fresh cilantro and parsley over the top, slice, and serve.

Note: Mexican oregano is not the same plant as Greek oregano or classic oregano. It is a tall plant that you could grow in your herb garden if you want to hunt for a source, but you can also find dried Mexican oregano at Penzeys or other online sources.

Pizza Margherita
Serves 4

Pizza Margherita is a classic Italian no-frills pizza named after Queen Margherita of Italy. (Bet you didn't know Italy once had a queen, did you?) Not much is as simple or as delicious as marinara sauce, flavorful cheese and some garlic, and fresh basil, which, incidentally, are the colors of the Italian flag.

> **1 recipe Basic Pizza dough (page 59)**
>
> **1 cup thick marinara sauce**
>
> **½ cup shredded fresh mozzarella cheese**
>
> **1 to 2 cloves garlic, minced finely**
>
> **8 leaves fresh basil, cut in chiffonade (see Note, page 32)**

Preheat the oven to 500°F about 15 minutes before baking.

With a rolling pin, roll the dough out into a fairly thin circle or rectangle, on a lightly floured surface.

Lay the dough on a baking sheet covered with parchment paper or a silicone baking mat with a light dusting of cornmeal. (If you're a pizza aficionado, you can use a pizza peel dusted with cornmeal, and a baking stone.) Let the dough rest for about 15 minutes.

Spread a thin coat of marinara sauce over the pizza. Evenly distribute the mozzarella and garlic. Bake for about 10 minutes, or until the crust is golden and the cheese is melted.

Remove from the oven, sprinkle the basil over the top, slice, and serve.

Four-Cheese and Three-Basil Pizza
Serves 4

This one is for those who love basil. Many nurseries offer several different kinds of basil in the spring. If you can find anise basil (also known as Thai basil), lemon basil, or cinnamon basil, by all means, plant it and use it. And if not, stick with Italian sweet basil, as it will taste just as good.

1 recipe Basic Pizza dough (page 59)

1 tomato, sliced thinly

¼ cup grated sharp Cheddar cheese

¼ cup grated smoked Gouda cheese

2 ounces goat cheese

¼ cup freshly grated Parmesan cheese

1 to 2 cloves garlic, minced finely

½ cup fresh basil, cut in chiffonade (see Note, page 32)

Preheat an oven to 500°F about 15 minutes before baking.

With a rolling pin, roll the dough out into a fairly thin circle or rectangle, on a lightly floured surface.

Lay the dough on a baking sheet covered with parchment paper or a silicone baking mat with a light dusting of cornmeal. (If you're a pizza aficionado, you can use a pizza peel dusted with cornmeal, and a baking stone.) Let the dough rest for about 15 minutes.

Arrange the tomato slices evenly over the surface of the pizza, then distribute the four cheeses and garlic on top. Bake for about 10 minutes, or until the crust is golden and the cheese is melted.

Remove from the oven, sprinkle the long strips of basil over the top, slice, and serve.

Harvest Focaccia with Grapes, Rosemary, and Parmesan
Serves 4 as a meal or 6 as an appetizer

In wine-drinking countries around the Western world, the grape harvest inevitably coincides with the harvest of grain. And partly as a result, bread and wine have been paired in celebration and ceremony. A traditional harvest focaccia represents the simplest and best of that tradition.

1 recipe Basic Pizza dough (page 59)

1½ cups grapes, cut in half

3 tablespoons fresh rosemary leaves, chopped coarsely

2 tablespoons fresh lemon zest, cut in strips

Pinch of salt

¼ cup freshly grated Parmesan or fontina cheese

¼ cup olive oil

Preheat the oven to 500°F about 15 minutes before baking.

Prepare your baking sheet or pizza stone and paddle and sprinkle with cornmeal.

Roll out the dough on a lightly floured surface to your desired shape and thickness, then place it on a pizza peel or baking sheet that has been lightly dusted with cornmeal. Cover and let rest and rise for 15 to 20 minutes. Remove the cover and use your fingers to dimple the dough all over.

Evenly distribute the grapes, rosemary, lemon zest, salt, and Parmesan over the surface of the dough. Drizzle with the olive oil. Bake for about 10 minutes, or until the crust is golden and the cheese is melted.

Remove from the oven, slice, and serve.

breads and
spreads

Artisan Whole Wheat Herb Breads: Grain and Garden Goodness

Several years ago, I enrolled in a week-long artisan bread baking class for professional bakers at the Culinary Institute of America in the Napa Valley. There are few places as beautiful or as full of serious foodies. The ovens are on the third story of this beautiful, old brick building, and the ambient temperature for most of that week was about 100°F. Everyone had to dress in regulation long, green-and-white checked pants and a long-sleeved white chef's jacket, buttoned all the way up. With the bread ovens cranked up to 500°F, I'm lucky I made it through the week. But make it, I did. And I came home with some new skills and a deepened love for bread and bakers. My particular "twist" on bread baking is that I like to do it, as often as possible, with wheat that I have just milled myself in my own kitchen. In the following recipes, you can use white flour or store-bought whole wheat flour, or a combination of both, but if you'd really like to learn something about grain, consider either buying freshly milled grain or grinding it at home yourself.

A word about yeast: Many professional bakers use SAF instant yeast, as it is very reliable and requires no proofing. You can add it right to your bread dough. Buy it from a good online source with a rapid turnover rate, such as King Arthur Flour. I also use and recommend Kitchen Resources' Dough Enhancer, a gluten-free enhancer that increases the rise of a whole-grain dough.

Basic Whole Wheat Artisan Loaf

Makes 1 loaf

Whether you make this bread from store-bought whole wheat flour or from whole wheat flour you've ground yourself at home, the results should yield a warm, delicious, sweet-smelling loaf. If you prefer a lighter loaf, you can substitute one or two cups of unbleached white bread flour for the whole wheat flour. Because I love the smell and flavor of freshly ground wheat, I often make this bread with no additions, and then slather it with just butter or spread or freshly made preserves.

3 cups whole wheat flour

2 teaspoons SAF instant yeast

1 teaspoon salt

1 teaspoon gluten or dough enhancer (optional)

1½ cups water or buttermilk (see Note)

2 tablespoons oil, plus more for coating

Place the flour, yeast, salt, and gluten, if using, in the work bowl of a food processor fitted with a dough blade and pulse a few times to mix.

Pour in the water and oil and let the machine run until the dough forms a clean ball in the processor. If your dough looks too wet and does not easily form a clean ball, turn off the machine for about 10 minutes and give the flour time to absorb some of the liquid. Then turn it back on again and let it run until the dough forms a clean ball. (Cuisinart recommends letting the machine run for 45 seconds after the ball is formed in the processor.)

Remove the dough from the food processor and shape it into a ball or disk. Place the dough in a large, lightly oiled bowl. Cover the bowl with a clean, damp dish towel.

continued

Let the dough rise in a warm spot until doubled in size, about 1½ hours. The time will vary with the temperature of your ingredients and the place you choose to rise dough. I often use my oven, which has a 100°F setting just perfect for raising bread dough.

Preheat the oven to 350°F and place a rack in the center.

Gently press the air out of the dough, then shape it into a loaf. Place the loaf in a well-oiled loaf pan and bake for 35 to 40 minutes, or until the loaf is golden brown. Alternatively, you can make a free-form loaf and let it rise and bake on a baking sheet covered with parchment paper or a silicone baking mat generously dusted with cornmeal.

Allow the bread to cool before removing from the pan.

Note: Depending upon the type of flour you are using, you may need to add a few extra tablespoons of water. Just remember that your visual cue is a nice, smooth ball of dough forming in the food processor.

Walnut, Apple, and Rosemary Loaf

Makes 1 loaf

This recipe makes a wonderful, rustic, flavorful, and aromatic loaf that, like all good bread, should be able to stand on its own with a good slab of butter or freshly made herbed cheese. I like to leave the skins on the organic apples for added flavor and texture, and I prefer to form the dough into a round and bake it on a baking sheet or baking stone.

3 cups whole wheat flour

2 teaspoons SAF instant yeast

1 teaspoon salt

1 teaspoon gluten or dough enhancer (optional)

3 tablespoons fresh rosemary leaves, chopped coarsely

1½ cups water or buttermilk (see Note)

2 tablespoons oil, preferably walnut, plus more for coating

1 cup Granny Smith apples, cored and cut into 1-inch pieces

1 cup walnuts, chopped coarsely

Place the flour, yeast, salt, gluten, if using, and rosemary in the work bowl of a food processor fitted with a dough blade and pulse a few times to mix.

Pour in the water and oil and let the machine run until the dough forms a clean ball in the processor. If your dough looks too wet and does not easily form a clean ball, turn off the machine for about 10 minutes and give the flour time to absorb some of the liquid. Then turn it back on again and let it run until the dough forms a clean ball. (Cuisinart recommends letting the machine run for 45 seconds after the ball is formed in the processor.)

continued

Remove the dough from the food processor, and knead in the apples and walnuts by hand. Shape the dough into a ball or disk, and place it in a large, lightly oiled bowl. Cover the bowl with a clean, damp dish towel.

Let the dough rise in a warm spot until doubled in size. I don't rush this one, because more complex flavors develop as the dough begins to rise. The time will vary with the temperature of your ingredients and the place you choose to rise dough. I often use my oven, which has a 100°F setting, just perfect for raising bread dough.

Preheat the oven to 350°F and place a rack in the center.

Gently press the air out of the dough, then shape it into a loaf. Place the loaf in a well-oiled loaf pan and bake for 35 to 40 minutes, or until the loaf is golden brown. Alternatively, you can make a free-form loaf and let it rise and bake on a baking sheet covered with parchment paper or a silicone baking sheet generously dusted with cornmeal.

Allow the bread to cool before removing from the pan or cutting.

Note: Depending upon the type of flour you are using, you may need to add a few extra tablespoons of water. Just remember that your visual cue is a nice, smooth ball of dough forming in the food processor.

Hazelnut, Dried Cherry, and Sage Round

Makes 1 round

This is a beautiful, delicious bread that may be eaten on its own or slathered with butter and toasted for breakfast.

> **3 cups whole wheat flour**
>
> **2 teaspoons SAF instant yeast**
>
> **1 teaspoon salt**
>
> **1 teaspoon gluten or dough enhancer (optional)**
>
> **1½ cups water or buttermilk (see Note)**
>
> **2 tablespoons oil, preferably hazelnut, plus more for coating**
>
> **½ cup dried cherries**
>
> **1 cup hazelnuts, chopped coarsely**
>
> **½ cup fresh sage leaves, chopped coarsely**

Place the flour, yeast, salt, and gluten, if using, in the work bowl of a food processor fitted with a dough blade and pulse a few times to mix.

Pour in the water and oil and let the machine run until the dough forms a clean ball in the processor. If your dough looks too wet and does not easily form a clean ball, turn off the machine for about 10 minutes and give the flour time to absorb some of the liquid. Then turn it back on again and let it run until the dough forms a clean ball. (Cuisinart recommends letting the machine run for 45 seconds after the ball is formed in the processor.)

Remove the dough from the food processor and knead in the cherries, hazelnuts, and sage by hand. Shape the dough into a ball or disk and place it in a large, lightly oiled bowl. Cover the bowl with a clean, damp dish towel.

continued

Let the dough rise in a warm spot until doubled in size, about 1½ hours. The time will vary with the temperature of your ingredients and the place you choose to rise dough. I often use my oven, which has a 100°F setting, just perfect for raising bread dough.

Preheat the oven to 350°F and place a rack in the center.

Gently press the air out of the dough, then shape it into a loaf. Place the loaf in a well-oiled loaf pan and bake for 35 to 40 minutes, or until the loaf is golden brown. Alternatively, you can make a free-form loaf and let it rise and bake on a baking sheet covered with parchment paper or a silicone baking sheet generously dusted with cornmeal.

Allow the bread to cool before removing from the pan.

Note: Depending upon the type of flour you are using, you may need to add a few extra tablespoons of water. Just remember that your visual cue is a nice, smooth ball of dough forming in the food processor.

Oregano, Cumin, and Cheese Loaf

Makes 1 loaf

I grew up in a conventional, middle-class American home, and at the time, no one ate wheat bread, and certainly no one I knew made bread at home. Spongy, white sandwich bread was the order of the day, so you can imagine what an awakening I had the day one of my college roommates brought home a loaf of bread that was laced with oregano and cheese. I went nuts, and decided I had to learn how to bake bread. This is my attempt at re-creating the loaf from sense memory, and it's not bad!

3 cups whole wheat flour

2 teaspoons SAF instant yeast

1 teaspoon salt

1 teaspoon gluten or dough enhancer (optional)

1½ cups water or buttermilk (see Note)

2 tablespoons oil, plus more for coating

1 cup cubed sharp Cheddar or Parmesan cheese (small cubes)

½ cup coarsely chopped fresh oregano leaves

1 teaspoon cumin seeds, ground coarsely

1 teaspoon coriander seeds, ground coarsely

Place the flour, yeast, salt, and gluten, if using, in the work bowl of a food processor fitted with a dough blade and pulse a few times to mix.

Pour in the water and oil and let the machine run until the dough forms a clean ball in the processor. If your dough looks too wet and does not easily form a clean ball, turn off the

continued

machine for about 10 minutes and give the flour time to absorb some of the liquid. Then turn it back on again and let it run until the dough forms a clean ball. (Cuisinart recommends letting the machine run for 45 seconds after the ball is formed in the processor.)

Remove the dough from the food processor and knead in the Cheddar, oregano, and cumin and coriander seeds. Shape the dough into a ball or disk and place it in a large, lightly oiled bowl. Cover the bowl with a clean, damp dish towel.

Let the dough rise in a warm spot until doubled in size, about 1½ hours. The time will vary with the temperature of your ingredients and the place you choose to rise dough. I often use my oven, which has a 100°F setting, just perfect for raising bread dough.

Preheat the oven to 350°F and place a rack in the center.

Gently press the air out of the dough, then shape it into a loaf. Place the loaf in a well-oiled loaf pan and bake for 35 to 40 minutes or until the loaf is golden brown. Alternatively, you can make a free-form loaf and let it rise and bake on a baking sheet covered with parchment paper or a silicone baking sheet generously dusted with cornmeal.

Allow the bread to cool before removing from the pan or cutting.

Note: Depending upon the type of flour you are using, you may need to add a few extra tablespoons of water. Just remember that your visual cue is a nice, smooth ball of dough forming in the food processor.

Scones: Garden Twists on a Classic Pastry

A favorite treat to myself when I lived in London some years ago was to take afternoon tea at one of the nicer hotels or tearooms. Good scones are as light as a feather and should easily come apart to hold your butter and preserves, but often the scones sold in American coffee shops could easily do double duty as doorstops.

Here's a hot tip for making good scones: The less you handle the dough, the lighter your scones will be. Do each step with the idea that you just want to mix ingredients, not give them a thorough workout. Using a food processor allows you to do this effortlessly and quickly.

Basic Scones
Makes 4 scones about 3 inches in diameter

I sometimes make these scones with whole wheat pastry flour, or sometimes with half pastry flour and half all-purpose white flour. Either way, they should be light and delicious and should be eaten as soon as they come out of the oven. Once you've mastered this basic recipe, you can improvise.

2 cups all-purpose flour

1 teaspoon baking soda

1 teaspoon cream of tartar

1 tablespoon sugar

½ teaspoon salt

½ cup (1 stick) cold butter, cut into 8 pieces

¾ cup buttermilk

½ cup dried currants (optional)

Butter and preserves, for serving

Preheat the oven to 400°F. Line a baking sheet with parchment paper or a silicone baking sheet.

In the work bowl of a food processor, combine the flour, baking soda, cream of tartar, sugar, and salt. Pulse to blend.

Add the cold butter. Turn on the machine and let it run until the butter is just blended in and the dough is the consistency of coarse cornmeal.

Turn off the machine and add the buttermilk and currants, if using, then pulse just long enough to blend the ingredients. Remove the dough from the processor and gently knead it in your hands, using just a few turns (no more than a dozen) to bring the dough together.

Lightly flour a cutting board. Roll out the dough until it is about 1 inch thick and cut it with a biscuit cutter or a water glass to form the scones. I use a large cutter, 3 inches in diameter.

Place the scones on the baking sheet and bake for 10 to 12 minutes, until golden brown.

Remove the scones from the oven. Let them cool a bit, then split them open and slather them with butter and preserves.

Savory Southwestern Nuggets with Jalapeño, Cilantro, and Coriander

Makes 4 scones about 3 inches in diameter

You can give a wonderful Southwestern flair to the basic scone recipe by adding jalapeños and Mexican oregano and slathering them with chile butter or a bit of butter flavored with sugar, lime juice, and zest.

1 ²/₃ cups all-purpose flour

¹/₃ cup cornmeal

1 ½ teaspoons baking powder

½ teaspoon baking soda

1 teaspoon salt

½ teaspoon ground coriander

½ teaspoon ground cumin

½ cup (1 stick) cold butter, cut into 8 pieces

¾ cup buttermilk

1 tablespoon coarsely chopped red bell pepper

1 tablespoon coarsely chopped jalapeño pepper

1 tablespoon chopped fresh oregano or Mexican oregano

Chile butter or lime butter, for serving (see Note)

Preheat the oven to 400°F. Line a baking sheet with parchment paper or a silicone baking sheet.

In the work bowl of a food processor, combine the flour, cornmeal, baking powder, baking soda, salt, coriander, and cumin. Pulse to blend.

Add the cold butter. Turn on the machine and let it run until the butter is just blended in and the dough is the consistency of coarse cornmeal.

Turn off the machine and add the buttermilk, both peppers, and oregano, then pulse just long enough to blend the ingredients. Remove the dough from the processor and gently knead it in your hands, using just a few turns (no more than a dozen) to bring the dough together.

Lightly flour a cutting board. Roll out the dough until it is about 1 inch thick and cut it with a biscuit cutter or a water glass to form the scones. I use a large cutter, 3 inches in diameter.

Place the scones on the baking sheet and bake for 10 to 12 minutes, until golden brown.

Remove the scones from the oven. Let them cool a bit, then split them open and slather them with chile or lime butter.

Note: To make chile or lime butter, start with a stick of room-temperature unsalted butter and add a pinch of chili powder, a few teaspoons of freshly squeezed lime juice, a teaspoon of lime zest, and salt to taste.

Sunday Scones with Dried Strawberries and Rosemary

Makes 4 scones about 3 inches in diameter

The only thing better than a plain, well-made scone is a scone with a few embellishments. In this case, dried fruit and herbs. You can top them with unsalted butter and honey, apricot or strawberry preserves, or clotted cream.

2 cups all-purpose flour

⅓ cup sugar

1 ½ teaspoons baking soda

½ teaspoon baking powder

½ teaspoon salt

½ cup (1 stick) cold butter, cut into pieces

¾ cup buttermilk

½ cup chopped dried strawberries or cranberries

1 tablespoon chopped fresh rosemary

Butter and preserves, for serving

Preheat the oven to 400°F. Line a baking sheet with parchment paper or a silicone baking sheet.

In the work bowl of a food processor, combine the flour, sugar, baking soda, baking powder and salt. Pulse to blend.

Add the cold butter. Turn on the machine and let it run until the butter is just blended in and the dough is the consistency of coarse cornmeal.

Turn off the machine and add the buttermilk, strawberries, and rosemary, then pulse just long enough to blend the ingredients. Remove the dough from the processor and gently knead it in your hands, using just a few turns (no more than a dozen) to bring the dough together.

Lightly flour a cutting board. Roll out the dough until it is about 1 inch thick and cut it with a biscuit cutter or a water glass to form the scones. I use a large cutter, 3 inches in diameter.

Place the scones on the baking sheet and bake for 10 to 12 minutes, until golden brown.

Remove the scones from the oven. Let them cool a bit, then split them open and slather with butter and preserves.

Spreads: Fresh and Easy Ways to Dress Up Bread

Many years ago, I had a summer job demonstrating food processors in a department store. Among the scripted recipes was one for a curry cheese spread that was just delicious. So delicious, in fact, that I began experimenting with variations on the theme of cream cheese, herbs, and spices, and I never really stopped. Here are a few simple recipes that I hope will set you on the road to experimentation with herbs and spreads.

Classic Basil Pesto

Makes about 1 ½ cups

Although a classic Italian pesto, or "paste," is made from basil, for our purposes, it can be made with any herb or combination of herbs. Here is a classic basil pesto that can be used as a spread or a delicious topping for pasta. If you use cilantro, try adding a few tablespoons of freshly squeezed lime or lemon juice.

4 cups fresh basil leaves

6 large cloves garlic, or more if desired

1 cup freshly grated Parmesan cheese

½ cup pine nuts or walnuts

1 cup high-quality olive oil, or a mixture of olive and vegetable oils

Salt and freshly ground black pepper

Combine the basil, garlic, Parmesan, and nuts in a food processor or blender. Pulse to mix and then chop them fine. Then, with the machine running, slowly add the olive oil through the feed tube. Season with salt and freshly ground pepper to taste.

Let the pesto stand for 5 minutes before serving.

Note: Although pesto is best served within the hour it is made, it can also be frozen in ice cube trays, then packed in plastic bags for later use.

Curry-Cilantro Cream Cheese Spread
Makes about 1 cup

I have made various versions of this delicious spread for many years, sometimes presenting it in a crock and sometimes rolling it into a ball covered with nuts. You can make it (or any of the spreads in this section) using commercial cream cheese or homemade yogurt cheese.

12 ounces cream cheese, at room temperature

1 cup shredded sharp Cheddar cheese

¼ cup dry sherry (optional)

2 teaspoons curry powder, or more as desired

¼ cup chopped walnuts, plus more for rolling (optional)

½ cup golden raisins or dried currants

¼ cup fresh cilantro leaves

Salt

Crackers or bread, for serving

Combine the cream cheese, Cheddar, sherry, if using, and curry powder in the work bowl of a food processor and blend well. Add the walnuts, raisins, and cilantro and pulse just until mixed. Be sure to leave plenty of texture. Season with salt to taste.

Spoon the mixture into a crock or roll it into a ball and cover it with walnuts, then refrigerate for at least 3 hours before serving on crackers or bread.

Making Herbed Mayo

Making mayonnaise at home could be one of the most simple yet satisfying tricks in the kitchen. More delicate than your average store-bought mayo, homemade mayo can be used as a base for a hearty potato salad, or delicate tea sandwiches, or even as a dip for fresh veggies. And it can be done in a matter of minutes, using a conventional blender, handheld immersion blender, or food processor.

In the work bowl of a food processor or blender, place 1 large egg, 1 teaspoon of salt, 1 tablespoon of white vinegar or freshly squeezed lemon juice, and, if you like, a teaspoon or more of Dijon mustard. With the machine running, slowly pour 1 cup of oil through the feed tube. The key word here is "slowly," because if you pour all of the oil in at once, you may not ever reach that thick, creamy texture you're looking for. You can add a single chopped fresh herb (dill, tarragon, or basil are three of my favorites), or a combination. If you like garlic, press a few fresh cloves into the mixture. I have, at times, used as many as six to eight cloves of garlic for a real kick.

This method yields about a cup of delicious homemade mayonnaise that will keep in the refrigerator for about a week, though I consider it best if used within a day or two.

If you are in a particularly grassroots kind of mood, try making your mayo the old-fashioned way. You'll need a large mortar and pestle. Place the egg, salt, and vinegar in the mortar and pound it into a paste. If you are adding garlic or mustard, this would be a good time to incorporate them. Add a cup of oil, two or three drops at a time, making sure to incorporate the oil after each pour before moving on. This may be time consuming but it's fun—so much so that you might consider giving each guest at a dinner party his or her own mortar, a glass of wine, and some ingredients, such as kalamata olives or roasted red peppers, to play with. Just pound away, drop by drop, until it begins to look and taste like mayo.

VEGAN ALTERNATIVE
Believe it or not, this stuff is great, especially when made with herbs from your own garden. Add more or less garlic to taste.

    2 (12-ounce) packages silken tofu

    2 tablespoons freshly squeezed lemon juice

    ¼ cup olive oil

    1 teaspoon salt

    4 cloves garlic, pressed (optional)

    1 tablespoon each of your favorite fresh herbs: dill, basil, marjoram, rosemary, chives, thyme, or whatever

Place the tofu, lemon juice, olive oil, and salt in the work bowl of a food processor or blender and blend until smooth. Press the cloves of fresh garlic (or more, if desired) into the sauce. Add as much of the fresh herbs of your choice as you like and pulse until blended.

Mock Boursin
Makes about 1 cup

Boursin is the brand name for a popular herbed cream cheese developed in France some years ago. I use it in twice-baked potatoes, as a spread on crackers, or even as a spread in sandwiches.

2 (8-ounce) packages cream cheese, or a combination of cream cheese and goat cheese

2 cloves garlic, pressed, or more as desired

Salt and freshly ground black pepper

2 tablespoons chopped fresh chives

2 tablespoons coarsely chopped fresh parsley

1 tablespoon fresh mixed herbs, such as tarragon, basil, chervil, or oregano

Place the cream cheese and garlic in the work bowl of a food processor and blend well. Add salt and freshly ground pepper to taste and blend.

Add the herbs and pulse until the herbs reach your desired consistency.

Pack the cheese into a crock or other serving container, cover, and refrigerate for several hours until the flavors have blended.

small
indulgences

Simple Sorbets: A Refreshing Palate Cleanser

A good sorbet can be a very versatile addition to your culinary bag of tricks. A fruit sorbet, for instance, makes a beautiful, light, delicious dessert. It's also a good way to use excess fruit from the garden or farmers' market. But a savory sorbet can be just as exciting, if not more so. The tomato sorbet in this chapter, for instance, can be served as a between-course palate cleanser, or you can allow it to "slush" on a hot day and enjoy a sort of iced gazpacho.

You may think that making sorbet requires an ice-cream or frozen yogurt maker, but I'm happy to tell you that isn't so. All you need is some frozen fruit or veggies, a bit of sugar (if you like), and a food processor.

You can use frozen fruit from the market, or you can freeze your own fruit in season. To freeze any fruit or veggie for use in sorbet, make sure the pieces are bite-size, then simply place them on a silicone- or parchment paper—lined baking sheet far enough apart from one another so they are not touching, then freeze them. When they are frozen solid, you can pack them into sealable plastic bags and return them to the freezer. Use them as you would any commercially frozen fruit or vegetable.

The amount of sugar needed will vary depending upon the type of fruit you are using, its degree of ripeness, and its intended use. And if you eat dairy products, try adding plain yogurt to the sorbet for a calcium boost and textural richness. Amounts of all ingredients are quite flexible, so don't be afraid to play around.

Basic Sweet Sorbet

Makes about 2 cups

Many years ago I was teaching cooking to children and looking for healthy, simple desserts. This basic fruit sorbet was the perfect thing. Kids loved it. It was easy to make. And it was delicious. You can use berries, as I have done here, or your own favorite fruit.

2 (12-ounce) packages frozen raspberries, strawberries, or a combination of both

¼ cup sugar, or more, if desired

Place the frozen fruit and sugar in the work bowl of a food processor. Pulse until the berries and sugar are reduced to a powder. Taste the mixture and add extra sugar if desired.

Let the machine run, stopping from time to time to scrape down the sides of the work bowl, until the mixture turns into a smooth sorbet. (Don't despair. It will turn to sorbet if you just keep at it!)

Scoop the sorbet into cups or cones, and enjoy. You can also pack it into a tightly sealed container and store it in the freezer for a day or two. Let it thaw a bit before serving.

Savory Cucumber Sorbet with Lemon and Rosemary
Makes about 2 cups

This refreshing sorbet is amazingly versatile. With little or no sugar added, it can be served as a between-course palate cleanser (as an accompaniment to the Tomato Sorbet, if you like). With a lot of sugar added, it becomes a light, refreshing dessert. I've used rosemary as the predominant herb, but you could just as easily use basil, dill (leaves and seeds), tarragon, or mint. Play around with amounts of sugar, salt, and lemon juice to find something that works perfectly for you or the occasion.

2 large cucumbers, peeled and cut into 1-inch pieces (about 4 cups), frozen

¼ cup freshly squeezed lemon juice

Salt

Sugar

2 tablespoons fresh rosemary leaves, chopped coarsely

Place the frozen cucumber pieces and lemon juice in the work bowl of a food processor. Pulse until the cucumber chunks are reduced to a fine powder, then add salt and sugar to taste.

Let the machine run, stopping from time to time to scrape down the sides of the work bowl, until the mixture turns into a smooth sorbet.

Add the rosemary leaves and pulse just until the rosemary is evenly distributed throughout the sorbet.

Scoop the sorbet into cups, and enjoy. You can also pack it into a tightly sealed container and store it in the freezer for a day or two. Let it thaw a bit before serving.

Pineapple Mint Sorbet
Makes about 2 cups

This is a refreshing, light, healthy dessert that requires the addition of very little or no sugar if you use a ripe pineapple. It's a great follow-up to Mexican or Indian foods, and can even be used as a break between courses to cool down the palate.

> **1 (16-ounce) bag frozen pineapple (about 4 cups of chunks), or 1 whole pineapple, trimmed, cut into chunks, and frozen (see Note)**
>
> **¼ to ½ cup sugar (optional)**
>
> **¼ cup fresh mint leaves, chopped coarsely**

Place the frozen pineapple pieces in the work bowl of a food processor. Taste to determine whether you need to add sugar, then pulse until the fruit is chopped into a fine powder. This may take a while.

Let the machine run steadily for short periods of time. Eventually, depending on how cold your fruit is and the size of the pieces, the mixture will begin to look more like a smooth sorbet than a powder.

Let the machine run, stopping from time to time to scrape down the sides of the work bowl, until the mixture turns into a smooth sorbet.

Add the chopped mint leaves at the last minute and run the machine only long enough to mix them in.

Scoop the sorbet into cups or cones, and enjoy. You can also scoop it into a container and pack it away in the freezer for a day or two. Let it thaw a bit before serving.

Note: If you are using fresh pineapple: Clean the pineapple thoroughly. Remove the peel and eyes. Cut into small pieces and freeze as directed on page 94.

Making Fresh Herb Teas

I first began experimenting with herb teas many years ago while still a college student. At the time, bulk dried herbs, even the more esoteric among them, were readily available in a couple of shops in town, and someone gave me a copy of the now classic book *Back to Eden* by Jethro Kloss. What followed was Potter's *Cyclopedia of Medicinal Herbs*. My roommates and neighbors became my guinea pigs, and I went from reading about herbs, to drinking herb teas, to growing them, to finally traveling to England to study herbal medicine.

But somewhere along the way, I found myself far more interested in drinking and eating my herbs than in approaching them strictly as medicines.

Maybe it was that delicate, fragrant, grassy cup of tilleul on my first visit to Paris. Or the thick mint tea in tiny demitasse cups served at the Paris Mosque, just across from the Jardin des Plantes. Or maybe that very first buttery, fresh, herb-laden omelet. All I know is that something about being in France, a country where people take their grub seriously, pushed me over the edge.

And after moving on from the wonderful herboristeries (herb pharmacies) of Paris, I came home and began making teas from fresh rather than dried herbs.

One of the most interesting aspects of fresh herb teas is their color. They are usually clear or a very pale green, and they only take on the familiar dark green color of dried herb teas if you boil them, which you should not do as they will quickly lose flavor and aroma. Steep them instead.

To concoct a pot of fresh herb tea, simply take about 1/4 cup of fresh herb leaves of your choice, twist them in your hands to liberate some of their oils, then stuff them into a prewarmed teapot. Pour in water just off the boil and let steep for about 10 minutes. The resulting tea should be clear or light green in color, and because the herbs are fresh, you may notice flavors and aromas that you never noticed before.

If you prefer a fresh herb iced tea, similar rules apply. Make a pot of herb tea, let it cool, and pour it over ice. Leftover tea often goes over ice and into my water bottle for yoga, hiking, or road trips.

Savory Tomato Sorbet with Oregano

Makes about 2 cups

Serve this savory sorbet icy cold as a between-course palate cleanser, or let it melt somewhat and serve it with a straw or spoon on a hot day, as a sort of gazpacho slush. You could just as easily use basil or rosemary, or you can try mixing herbs and spices for different effects. Leave the skins on the organic tomatoes for additional color, flavor, and nutrients.

4 fairly firm tomatoes, each cut into 8 pieces (about 4 cups), frozen

½ teaspoon cumin seeds, crushed

½ teaspoon coriander seeds, crushed

2 teaspoons freshly squeezed lemon juice

Salt

Freshly ground black pepper

¼ cup fresh oregano leaves, chopped coarsely

Place the frozen tomato pieces, crushed seeds, and lemon juice in the work bowl of a food processor. Pulse to break up the tomato pieces, then continue pulsing until they are reduced to a powder.

Add salt and freshly ground pepper to taste. Let the machine run, stopping from time to time to scrape down the sides of the work bowl, until the mixture turns into a smooth sorbet.

Add the oregano leaves and pulse a few times until they are thoroughly mixed in.

Scoop the sorbet into cups, and enjoy. You can also scoop it into a container and pack it away in the freezer for a day or two. Let it thaw a bit before serving.

Mini Cheesecakes: Small Bites with Big Flavor

Cheesecake can make a very versatile addition to your cooking repertoire. When served without the addition of sugar they make a delicious
lunch, first course, or appetizer. And there is no end to the dessert
possibilities when you add sugar, fresh fruit, and garden-fresh herbs.

Basic Cheesecake with Berries
Serves 4

This is a simple, lightly sweetened cheesecake that I like to serve with fresh strawberries or raspberry sauce. I have sized the recipe for four individual-size cheesecakes, rather than one large cake. Use low-fat cream cheese or Neufchâtel cheese (about one-third less fat than regular cream cheese) to lower the calorie content.

Crust

6 graham crackers

1 tablespoon unsalted butter

Filling

3 (8-ounce) packages cream cheese, at room temperature

1 cup sour cream

½ cup sugar

1 tablespoon vanilla extract

3 large eggs

Strawberries or raspberries, for garnishing

Preheat the oven to 325°F and place a rack in the center.

Make the crust: Combine the graham crackers and butter in a food processor and process until they form a coarse, even powder. Divide the mixture among four prepared mini (4 ½-inch) springform pans and press firmly into the bottom of the pans.

continued

Make the filling: Place the cream cheese, sour cream, sugar, and vanilla in the work bowl of a food processor and let the machine run until the ingredients are thoroughly mixed. Add the eggs and mix in thoroughly.

Divide the filling among the four pans, and gently tap each pan on a cutting board or countertop to evenly distribute the filling and release any air bubbles.

Place the pans on a rimmed baking sheet and bake for about 10 minutes, or just until set, with the edges ever-so-slightly puffed. Do not overbake.

Transfer the cheesecakes to a wire rack and let cool for about 45 minutes, then refrigerate for at least 6 hours. Unmold each cheesecake on a serving plate and garnish with fresh berries.

Savory Cheesecakes with Thyme, Sage, and Rosemary

Serves 4

These delicious, small, savory, herb-filled cheesecakes can be served warm or cold. Pair them with a salad for lunch, or make them as a first course, or as a small, spreadable appetizer. You can go for a monotone approach with just one herb, such as rosemary, or take a multifaceted approach, such as in this recipe, which combines three of the so-called resinous herbs (see page xiv). You can also vary the cheeses, if you like, using varieties that complement your chosen herbs.

Crust

6 whole-grain crackers

1 tablespoon unsalted butter

¼ cup chopped walnuts or almonds

Filling

2 (8-ounce) packages cream cheese, at room temperature

1 (11-ounce) package goat cheese

2 ounces feta cheese

½ cup grated sharp Cheddar cheese

1 cup sour cream

6 cloves garlic

½ teaspoon coarsely chopped fresh thyme

½ teaspoon coarsely chopped fresh sage

½ teaspoon coarsely chopped fresh rosemary leaves

3 large eggs

continued

Preheat the oven to 325°F and place a rack in the center.

Make the crust: Combine the crackers, butter, and walnuts in the work bowl of a food processor and process until they form a coarse, even powder. Divide the mixture among four mini (4½-inch) springform pans and press firmly into the bottom of the pans.

Make the filling: Place all four cheeses, the sour cream, garlic, and herbs in the work bowl of a food processor and let the machine run until the ingredients are thoroughly mixed. Add the eggs and mix well.

Divide the filling among the four pans, and gently tap each pan on a cutting board or countertop to evenly distribute the filling and release any air bubbles.

Place the pans on a rimmed baking sheet and bake for about 10 minutes, or just until set, with the edges ever-so-slightly puffed. Do not overbake.

Transfer the cheesecakes to a wire rack and let cool for a few minutes. Either serve warm (not hot, but warm) over a salad, or let cool completely, and then cover and refrigerate for at least 5 hours to serve cold.

Lemon-Rosemary Cheesecakes
Serves 4

Lemon and rosemary are such a classic combination, and especially appropriate for a spring or summer lunch or dinner. You may wish to vary the amounts of the rosemary, lemon juice, and zest, but this is the way I like it.

Crust

6 to 8 shortbread cookies

1 tablespoon unsalted butter

Filling

3 (8-ounce) packages cream cheese, at room temperature

½ cup sugar

1 tablespoon freshly squeezed lemon juice

2 teaspoons lemon zest

1 cup sour cream

3 large eggs

2 teaspoons rosemary leaves, chopped coarsely

Strawberries or raspberries, for garnishing

Preheat the oven to 325°F and place a rack in the center.

Make the crust: Combine the shortbread cookies and butter in the work bowl of a food processor and process until they form a coarse, even powder. Divide the mixture among four mini (4½-inch) springform pans and press firmly into the bottom of the pans.

continued

Make the filling: Place the cream cheese, sugar, lemon juice and zest, and sour cream in the work bowl of a food processor and let the machine run until the ingredients are thoroughly mixed. Then add the eggs and beat in thoroughly. Add the rosemary leaves and pulse until they are the desired size and texture.

Divide the filling evenly among the four pans, and gently tap each pan on a cutting board or countertop to evenly distribute the filling and release any air bubbles.

Place the pans on a rimmed baking sheet and bake for about 10 minutes, or just until set, with edges ever-so-slightly puffed. Do not overbake.

Transfer the cheesecakes to a wire rack and let cool for about 45 minutes, then refrigerate for at least 6 hours. Unmold each cheesecake on a serving plate and garnish with fresh berries.

Chocolate Walnut Peppermint Cheesecakes

Serves 4

Over the years, I've found that many different kinds of mints complement chocolate, but because of its menthol content, I like peppermint the best. Use spearmint, orange bergamot mint, or whatever you like, but peppermint gives the most stunning flavor contrast with the chocolate.

Crust

6 chocolate mint cookies, such as Thin Mints, crushed

1 tablespoon unsalted butter

Filling

8 ounces (about 1 cup) semisweet chocolate chips

3 (8-ounce) packages cream cheese, at room temperature

½ cup sugar

1 cup sour cream

3 large eggs

1 cup walnuts, chopped coarsely

¼ cup coarsely chopped fresh peppermint leaves

Preheat the oven to 325°F and place a rack in the center.

Make the crust: Combine the cookies and butter in the work bowl of a food processor and process until they form a coarse, even powder. Divide the mixture among four mini (4 ½-inch) springform pans and press firmly into the bottom of the pans.

continued

Make the filling: Place the chocolate chips in a large, microwave-safe measuring cup and microwave at 100 percent power for about 1 minute. The chips will not appear to be melted, but stir them with a fork and see what happens. If they are still not quite melted, return them to the microwave for 30-second increments (so as not to overcook) until they are thoroughly melted.

Combine the melted chocolate, cream cheese, sugar, and sour cream in the work bowl of a food processor and let the machine run until the mixture is relatively light and fluffy. Add the eggs and mix well. Stir in the walnuts.

Divide the filling among the four pans, and gently tap each pan on a cutting board or countertop to evenly distribute the filling and release any air bubbles.

Place the pans on a rimmed baking sheet and bake for about 10 minutes, or just until set, with the edges ever-so-slightly puffed. Do not overbake.

Transfer the cheesecakes to a wire rack and let cool for about 45 minutes, then refrigerate for at least 6 hours. Unmold each cheesecake on a serving plate. Garnish with coarsely chopped fresh peppermint leaves.

Metric Conversions and Equivalents

Metric Conversion Formulas

To convert	Multiply
Ounces to grams	Ounces by 28.35
Pounds to kilograms	Pounds by 0.454
Teaspoons to milliliters	Teaspoons by 4.93
Tablespoons to milliliters	Tablespoons by 14.79
Fluid ounces to milliliters	Fluid ounces by 29.57
Cups to milliliters	Cups by 236.59
Cups to liters	Cups by 0.236
Quarts to liters	Quarts by 0.946
Inches to centimeters	Inches by 2.54

Approximate Metric Equivalents

Volume

¼ teaspoon	1 milliliter
½ teaspoon	2.5 milliliters
¾ teaspoon	4 milliliters
1 teaspoon	5 milliliters
1 tablespoon (½ fluid ounce)	15 milliliters
¼ cup	60 milliliters
⅓ cup	80 milliliters
½ cup (4 fluid ounces)	120 milliliters
⅔ cup	160 milliliters
¾ cup	180 milliliters
1 cup (8 fluid ounces)	240 milliliters
2 cups (1 pint)	460 milliliters
3 cups	700 milliliters

Weight

1 ounce	28 grams
2 ounces	57 grams
4 ounces (¼ pound)	113 grams
5 ounces	142 grams
6 ounces	170 grams
7 ounces	198 grams
8 ounces (½ pound)	227 grams
16 ounces (1 pound)	454 grams

Length

¼ inch	6 millimeters
½ inch	1.25 centimeters
1 inch	2.5 centimeters
4 inches	10 centimeters
6 inches	15.25 centimeters
12 inches (1 foot)	30 centimeters

Oven Temperatures

To convert Fahrenheit to Celsius, subtract 32 from Fahrenheit, multiply the result by 5, then divide by 9.

description	fahrenheit	celsius	british gas mark
Very cool	200°	95	0
Very cool	225°	110°	¼
Very cool	250°	120°	½
Cool	275°	135°	1
Cool	300°	150°	2
Warm	325°	165°	3
Moderate	350°	175°	4
Moderately hot	375°	190°	5
Fairly hot	400°	200°	6
Hot	425°	220°	7
Very hot	450°	230°	8
Very hot	475°	245°	9

Common Ingredients and Their Approximate Equivalents

1 cup uncooked rice = 225 grams
1 cup all-purpose flour = 140 grams
1 stick butter (4 ounces • ½ cup • 8 tablespoons) = 110 grams
1 cup butter (8 ounces • 2 sticks • 16 tablespoons) = 220 grams
1 cup brown sugar, firmly packed = 225 grams
1 cup granulated sugar = 200 grams

Information compiled from a variety of sources, including *Recipes into Type* by Joan Whitman and Dolores Simon (Newton, MA: Biscuit Books, 2000); *The New Food Lover's Companion* by Sharon Tyler Herbst (Hauppauge, NY: Barron's, 1995); and *Rosemary Brown's Big Kitchen Instruction Book* (Kansas City, MO: Andrews McMeel, 1998).

Index